JOEY MERLINO THE LAST MOB STAR

CW01500605

From Philadelphia's Streets to Netflix Screens The Rise, Fall, and Reinvention of America's Flashiest Wiseguy

by

Eldon A. Jessen

Table of Contents

Introduction

Between Loyalty and Legend

There are few figures in modern American history who blur the line between myth and man quite like Joey Merlino. For decades, his name has carried both infamy and intrigue a blend of South Philadelphia charm, underworld rumor, and pop-culture fascination that refuses to fade. To some, he is the last remnant of a bygone era of loyalty, code, and charisma. To others, he is a cautionary tale a man who learned too late that notoriety can be both currency and curse. But to everyone who's ever heard of him, Joey Merlino represents something rare: a gangster who became a star.

In every age, America has been drawn to rebels who live on their own terms. From Wild West outlaws to Wall Street mavericks, the culture rewards defiance almost as much as it condemns it. In that sense, Joey Merlino was made for his time. Born in South Philadelphia, a place where loyalty ran as deep as the neighborhood roots, Joey came of age in a world defined by family, pride, and quiet power. His father, Salvatore "Chuckie" Merlino, was a known name in organized circles and from an early age, Joey was surrounded by the whispers and glamour of "the life." Yet unlike the old-school mobsters who preferred the shadows, Joey stepped into the light.

By the 1990s, he was no longer just a figure in the underworld he was a fixture in the headlines. Reporters followed him leaving court, fans asked for photos, and restaurants saved him a seat. He dressed sharp, smiled for cameras, and seemed to relish the media frenzy that most mob figures ran from. He didn't hide. He hosted charity events. He attended nightclubs. He gave interviews. To some, it looked like arrogance; to others, confidence. To everyone watching, it looked like something new a celebrity mobster.

But behind the flash and confidence, there was always a dangerous reality. The Philadelphia Mafia, long one of the most turbulent crime families in America, was undergoing one of its most violent eras. The 1990s brought a brutal internal conflict between John Stanfa, the traditional Sicilian-born boss, and a younger, more flamboyant challenger Joey Merlino. The streets turned bloody, alliances shifted, and the city that once feared the mob now treated it like a running news story. Through it all, Joey became the face of an empire in transition: old codes colliding with a new culture of visibility.

What makes Merlino's story so unique is not only how far he rose, but how deliberately he redefined what power looked like. He embodied the paradox of modern fame using charm and openness as armor in a world that demanded silence. He would be photographed in expensive suits one day and appear in handcuffs the next, smiling for the cameras either way. He understood image as strategy long before social media made it commonplace.

Yet every rise invites a reckoning. Federal agents never stopped watching. Wiretaps, surveillance, and informants followed him through the years. The same charisma that made him magnetic to the public made him vulnerable to betrayal. By the early 2000s, Merlino had become both the public face and the hunted target of the Philadelphia mob. Trials and convictions followed, and eventually, prison time. Still, even behind bars, his legend grew. His name remained shorthand for a lost kind of underworld glamor one that mixed style with danger and respect with spectacle.

When he emerged from prison, many expected him to fade into anonymity. Instead, Joey Merlino did what he had always done best: he adapted. He returned to Philadelphia and later Florida, claiming to have left "the life" behind, but never fully escaping the fascination that followed him. He opened *Skinny Joey's Cheesesteaks*, a restaurant that turned his nickname into a brand. He appeared on podcasts, spoke candidly about his past, and leaned into the very persona that once put him under scrutiny.

And now, with the release of Netflix's *Mob War: Philadelphia vs. The Mafia* in 2025, the world is once again talking about Joey Merlino. For a new generation, he isn't just a figure from a newspaper headline he's a streaming phenomenon, a character larger than life. The documentary brings back the tension, glamour, and contradictions of an era that refuses to die. But it also raises a question that has followed Joey for years: *was he a criminal, or a creation of the media?*

This book doesn't glorify crime, nor does it sanitize history. Instead, it examines a life lived at full volume a portrait of a man who played both sides of fame and infamy with startling precision. It explores how Joey Merlino became a reflection of the times: the last in a line of mobsters who understood that image can be as powerful as influence, that perception can shape reality.

Through meticulous research, interviews, and firsthand accounts, *Joey Merlino: The Last Mob Star* traces the story from the narrow streets of South Philadelphia to the modern world of streaming fame and entrepreneurial reinvention. It examines how Joey's charisma and contradictions made him both beloved and controversial a man who claimed to leave "the life" yet remained forever bound to it by name and narrative.

In the end, the goal is not to judge Joey Merlino, but to understand him. To see how one man, caught between tradition and transformation, became the symbol of an era's final act when the Mafia traded secrecy for celebrity, and silence for spectacle. His story is not only about crime; it's about identity, resilience, and reinvention in a culture obsessed with notoriety.

As the lights fade and the Netflix credits roll, one truth remains: Joey Merlino never stopped being watched. Whether as a leader, a legend, or a lingering mystery, he continues to capture the imagination of a public that cannot look away.

And perhaps that is the secret behind every myth not the deeds themselves, but the performance that turns them into something unforgettable. Joey Merlino understood that better than anyone.

This is his story.

Chapter 1

South Philly Roots

South Philadelphia in the 1960s was more than a collection of streets; it was a living heartbeat. Narrow brick row houses leaned shoulder to shoulder like old friends sharing secrets, and every block seemed to carry the sound of conversation, laughter, and the faint rhythm of an accordion echoing from a radio left open in a kitchen window. On summer nights, mothers pulled chairs out onto the sidewalks, children played stickball until the streetlights came on, and the aroma of garlic and simmering tomatoes drifted from one home to another. Life was small, loud, and deeply rooted in pride.

For the families who settled there after crossing oceans from southern Italy, South Philly offered belonging. Everyone knew each other's names, histories, and habits. The corner store owner was also the godfather to someone's child; the tailor knew the secrets of every household by the cut of a suit. Loyalty wasn't a rule it was the air people breathed. To belong meant to protect one another and to carry the stories of those who came before.

Into this world came Joseph Merlino, a boy whose charm seemed to light up even the narrowest alleyway. His childhood was colored by the scent of homemade bread and the sound of church bells that marked both joy and duty. His mother kept the home warm and ordered, her faith steady as the rosary beads she kept beside her bed. His father, Salvatore Merlino, known to neighbors as "Chuckie," was a figure of confidence and strength the kind of man who walked with purpose and whose word carried weight.

To a child, that weight meant mystery. Joey often sensed that his father's influence extended beyond ordinary neighborhood respect. Men spoke to him quietly, shook his hand firmly, and moved aside when he passed. Yet at home, Salvatore could be tender, encouraging his sons to stand tall, look people in the eye, and never forget where they came from. The lesson was simple but lasting: *honor the family name and protect those you love.*

The Merlino home, like many in South Philadelphia, was humble but full of life. Joey's earliest memories were of Sunday gatherings long tables stretching across the dining room, plates piled high, voices rising and falling like music. The conversations mixed old Italian phrases with American slang, and children darted between chairs, stealing meatballs from bowls while the adults debated politics or baseball. Food was never just food; it was love, pride, and storytelling all in one.

The church stood at the center of that community. Every milestone baptisms, weddings, funerals happened beneath its stone arches. The priest knew every family by name, and attendance on Sunday was not a choice but an expectation. Faith wove itself into daily life. Joey watched how his mother's devotion steadied her, how the flicker of a candle or the scent of incense could soften a hard week. Even as he grew older and began questioning authority, that quiet image of faith stayed somewhere inside him.

South Philadelphia was also a place of constant contrast laughter alongside hardship, compassion alongside fear. The neighborhood was safe for those who belonged, but outsiders rarely lingered. Respect was currency, and gossip could turn into consequence. For young Joey, that sense of unwritten order fascinated him. He saw how grown men could settle disputes with a look or a quiet word. He noticed who spoke first and who listened. The streets taught lessons no classroom ever could about trust, posture, and timing.

At school, Joey was bright, restless, and quick to smile. Teachers sometimes described him as charming but distracted. He preferred stories to equations, conversation to conformity. There was an energy about him an urge to move faster than the world around him. When he walked home from class, he would slow near the corner where older men gathered outside cafés, playing cards or sipping espresso. They wore crisp shirts, even on humid days, and spoke softly in sentences that ended in laughter or silence, depending on who was listening.

Those moments stirred something in him curiosity mixed with admiration. These were men who carried themselves with unspoken confidence. They looked ordinary but seemed untouchable. Joey didn't yet understand the world they inhabited, but he recognized power when he saw it. He felt drawn to it, the way some children feel drawn to the stage or the sea.

Still, his youth was not shadowed by danger; it was defined by discovery. He rode his bicycle through the narrow lanes, played stickball in the street, and spent evenings helping his mother in the kitchen, sneaking bites of sauce before she could scold him. Life was tight but colorful. There were few luxuries, but there was pride in every effort. Families took care of one another, and neighbors watched each other's children as if they were their own.

As adolescence crept in, so did the first signs of tension. The city was changing. Factories closed, opportunities shrank, and the sons of immigrant families looked for ways to hold on to a sense of control. Some joined unions, others pursued trades, and a few found quicker, riskier paths to respect. Joey observed all of it. He saw that in his neighborhood, survival wasn't about strength alone it was about perception, loyalty, and daring.

He had inherited his father's confidence and his mother's persistence. That combination made him magnetic. People noticed when he walked into a room; his grin could ease a disagreement or start a conversation. Yet beneath that lightness was determination. He wanted to be more than a face in the crowd. He wanted to matter.

On warm nights, he and his friends would gather on stoops, talking about cars they couldn't yet afford and futures they hadn't yet defined. The streetlights cast long shadows across the pavement, and every so often, a sleek black car would glide down the block, slowing near a corner café before disappearing again. To most boys, it was nothing. To Joey, it was a reminder that somewhere beyond the ordinary rhythm of their days, another world existed one ruled by quiet authority, one that demanded both nerve and intelligence.

The lessons of his upbringing shaped how he saw that world. His parents taught him to stand by his word. His community taught him that silence was sometimes stronger than speech. Every handshake carried meaning; every favor came with memory. Joey absorbed these lessons like instinct. He began to understand that success in any form in business, in friendship, in life depended on who you trusted and how you carried yourself.

Through his teenage years, South Philadelphia became both a comfort and a challenge. He loved its closeness but felt its limits. Opportunity rarely reached beyond the same familiar streets. Those who dreamed of something larger often left; those who stayed learned to make their own kind of mark. Joey chose the latter. His world was built on presence showing up, being seen, and earning respect.

By the time he entered early adulthood, Joey had developed a reputation for confidence beyond his years. He spoke with the ease of someone twice his age, yet he never lost the boyish energy that made people want to follow his lead. He could defuse tension with a joke or ignite loyalty with a few sincere words. To friends, he was dependable. To elders, he was promising. To himself, he was just beginning.

Philadelphia, with all its grit and grace, molded him. The scent of fresh bread on Ninth Street, the clang of the trolley lines, the echo of a crowd at a local ballgame these became the background music of his young life. Every sound and scent carried memory: the thump of a newspaper hitting the doorstep at dawn, the voice of a vendor shouting about peaches or cigars, the steady hum of a radio playing Italian love songs through an open window. All of it formed a rhythm that would stay with him long after he left those streets.

But even in those years, the city carried stories of struggle. Unemployment, unrest, and political scandals made headlines. To survive was to adapt, and Joey watched how the older generation did just that. Some turned inward, focusing on family and faith; others sought control in less conventional ways. He learned early that power was not always granted sometimes it was simply taken by those bold enough to claim it.

Joey's faith in himself grew alongside that realization. He admired the discipline of his father, the resilience of his mother, and the courage of his neighbors who faced each day with quiet pride. He understood that the strength of South Philadelphia was not in its wealth but in its unity in the way people stood together through hardship. That solidarity would become one of the guiding forces of his life, shaping his choices, friendships, and the loyalty he demanded in return.

Even as the years carried him further from childhood, the spirit of those streets stayed inside him. Whenever he visited home, the same faces greeted him with warmth, the same smells drifted from kitchen windows, and the same church bells rang over the rooftops. No matter how far he would one day travel or how much his name would come to mean this was where he learned who he was.

In South Philadelphia, reputation was everything. A man's word was his bond, and a broken promise could echo louder than a shout. That principle would guide Joey throughout his life, shaping his relationships and his resilience. Whether facing admiration or adversity, he carried the imprint of those early lessons that family, faith, and loyalty could endure even when the world turned against you.

The neighborhood that raised him never truly left him. Its rhythm lived in his voice, its pride in his posture. Beneath the surface charm that would later captivate reporters and onlookers, there remained that boy from Ninth Street curious, bold, and unafraid to stand out.

South Philadelphia was more than geography; it was character. It demanded respect, but it also gave belonging. It was a place that taught the meaning of resilience, the beauty of community, and the quiet dignity of standing your ground. In those lessons lay the roots of everything Joey Merlino would become the confidence, the charisma, and the unshakable sense of self that would carry him through triumph and turmoil alike.

Before the headlines, before the fame, before the name "Skinny Joey" echoed beyond the city's borders, there was this: a boy walking home through narrow streets lined with voices and history, a boy who learned early that power begins not with strength but with presence. The warmth of that community, the watchful eyes of neighbors, and the heartbeat of a neighborhood built on faith and pride all of it formed the foundation of a life that would one day capture the world's attention.

That foundation, with its blend of loyalty, charm, and fire, would become both his armor and his legacy. South Philadelphia made Joey Merlino who he was and it would remain, always, the one place that truly understood him.

Chapter 2

Lessons in Loyalty

Loyalty was not a lesson Joey Merlino learned from books it was something that lived and breathed in his home, his neighborhood, and the quiet conversations that carried more meaning than the words themselves. In South Philadelphia, loyalty wasn't just expected; it was the single thread that held families, friendships, and reputations together. A person's worth could be measured not by what they owned, but by whom they stood beside when times grew hard.

Joey's earliest understanding of the word came from his father's steady example. Salvatore "Chuckie" Merlino was a man who never spoke carelessly. When he promised to do something, he did it, and when he warned someone not to cross a line, no one dared to test him twice. People came to their door with quiet respect, sometimes fear, but always trust. Joey noticed that even in moments of silence, his father's presence commanded attention. He could diffuse a tense conversation with a calm tone, yet there was always a sense that beneath that calm lived unspoken power.

At the dinner table, loyalty was served alongside every meal. His mother would remind her sons that family came before pride, before anger, before ambition. "No matter what happens out there," she often said, "you look after your own." To her, loyalty was love in its purest form the willingness to sacrifice comfort for the sake of someone else's dignity. Joey carried that lesson like an invisible tattoo.

Yet, for a boy so full of energy and charm, loyalty also meant conflict. He had a streak of rebellion that could not be contained by rules alone. While he respected authority at home, he often tested it everywhere else. Teachers admired his intelligence but struggled to contain his restlessness. He could disarm them with humor one moment and challenge their patience the next. It wasn't disrespect; it was curiosity an instinct to see where boundaries truly lay.

Outside the classroom, he moved through the neighborhood with the confidence of someone older. His friends admired his ease, how he could turn a reprimand into a joke or convince a skeptical shop owner to trust him with a few extra minutes of credit. He was bold but not reckless. There was calculation in his charm an understanding that people respond to warmth faster than they do to fear.

That instinct, unrefined but powerful, drew people toward him. By his early teens, Joey had a small circle of friends who followed his lead in almost everything. They looked up to him not because he demanded it, but because he earned it. He protected them when older boys tried to intimidate, and when arguments broke out, his voice usually carried the final word. Loyalty was the glue of that small group, and betrayal even something as minor as breaking a promise was treated with seriousness.

In South Philadelphia, words carried weight. Gossip could build or break reputations. Joey learned early that silence was its own kind of power. He didn't repeat what he heard, and that simple act made people trust him. Even as a teenager, he understood that keeping a secret was not only a courtesy it was a currency.

His father's name carried influence, but Joey wanted respect on his own terms. He watched how older men conducted themselves the ones who commanded quiet in a room simply by being present. He noticed that those who lasted longest in life, whether in business or the neighborhood, were the ones who understood loyalty's double edge: it could protect you, but it could also trap you. Once someone offered their allegiance, it was nearly impossible to withdraw without consequence.

That lesson took on meaning one afternoon when a dispute broke out near a corner café. Joey, barely in his mid-teens, was with two friends when a man confronted another over money owed. The voices rose, chairs scraped the pavement, and a crowd began to form. Most bystanders stayed back, unwilling to get involved. Joey, however, stepped forward. He said nothing but positioned himself near his friends, close enough that the angry men noticed. It was a small gesture an unspoken signal that he would not run if things turned rough. The fight dissolved soon after, but the memory stuck. One of the older men later told Joey, "You don't talk much, kid, but when you stand somewhere, people know you mean it."

It was a compliment that mattered more than any praise from school or home. That was the day he began to understand that loyalty wasn't declared it was proven through presence.

Through his teenage years, the Merlino household was a place of both discipline and affection. His mother's cooking drew relatives and neighbors like a magnet, and laughter often filled the kitchen. Yet beneath the warmth lingered the quiet awareness that their family was different. His father's world reached into corners that Joey didn't fully see but could sense. When guests came to the house, the conversations often shifted when the children entered the room. Certain names were never spoken, and certain questions were never asked twice.

To Joey, this wasn't fear it was respect. Every home in South Philadelphia had its unspoken rules, and theirs were simply part of life. He understood that not everything needed explaining; some things were simply understood.

The older he grew, the more he noticed how those invisible rules shaped the community. Loyalty didn't just apply to families; it extended to friendships, neighborhoods, even churches. It was the foundation that kept the area strong when the outside world began to change. The factories that once offered steady work were closing, and many families struggled to stay afloat. Through all of it, the sense of unity in South Philly held firm. People leaned on one another. They shared meals, traded favors, and stood together when hardship came knocking.

Joey admired that resilience. He also admired the quiet strength of those who protected it. Every community had men who looked after their own not with badges or titles, but with presence and persuasion. Joey didn't yet understand the complexities of those roles, but he recognized their power. And power, to him, was something earned through trust.

By seventeen, he had learned how to read people almost instinctively. He could sense sincerity, spot hesitation, and tell when someone was bluffing. Friends came to him for advice, small matters at first a disagreement, a misunderstanding, a favor. He handled each with surprising calm, preferring to talk rather than fight. It wasn't about avoiding conflict; it was about control. He learned that sometimes, the most loyal act was to stop someone from making a mistake that could cost them later.

But even as Joey matured, his rebellious streak remained. He hated being underestimated. He disliked being told to "wait his turn." If loyalty was the code, he wanted to live by it his own way direct, fearless, and unyielding. That confidence, while magnetic, sometimes caused friction with older men who valued tradition and patience. Joey respected them, but he also believed respect was a two-way street. He had little tolerance for hypocrisy, and even less for betrayal.

That intensity would become both his gift and his curse.

One evening, during a family gathering, Joey overheard two older relatives arguing quietly in the next room. Their voices were low, but the word "loyalty" kept repeating sharp, heavy, final. Though he couldn't catch every sentence, the tone was enough to freeze him. He realized that for adults in his world, loyalty wasn't just emotional; it was existential. It could save lives or end them. That realization sat heavily with him, yet it also clarified something: loyalty without honesty was hollow.

From that moment, Joey treated promises as sacred. He avoided making them lightly. If he said he would do something, he did it. That reputation followed him everywhere through his early jobs, his friendships, and even the smallest interactions on the street. People began to trust him not because of his name, but because of his consistency.

In the neighborhood, that kind of reliability carried more weight than ambition. When someone could be counted on, they were worth keeping close. Joey's circle of friends deepened, bound by years of shared memories, favors, and laughter. They celebrated each other's milestones, stood guard when trouble loomed, and never forgot who was there when it mattered.

Those friendships shaped him as much as his family did. They gave him a sense of belonging that was both emotional and strategic. Trust became his compass. Even decades later, through storms of fame and scrutiny, that principle would never leave him.

Still, loyalty demanded sacrifice. Joey learned that it wasn't always comfortable or fair. There were times he stood by someone only to be disappointed, moments when silence cost him more than truth would have. Yet even then, he didn't waver. He believed that betrayal, no matter how small, had a ripple effect that could shatter everything around it.

That belief hardened into habit.

By the time his late teens arrived, Joey's personality was fully formed charming yet cautious, sociable yet guarded. He knew how to smile without revealing too much, how to listen without promising agreement. Those traits would later define his public image, but they were born here, in the neighborhood that raised him on lessons of loyalty.

South Philadelphia's narrow streets taught their own curriculum one built on observation, not instruction. Joey learned that a man's reputation wasn't built overnight; it was earned through hundreds of small actions, each one proving consistency. He saw how quickly trust could be broken and how hard it was to rebuild. He watched people rise through dedication and fall through deceit. Every lesson came quietly, but it stuck like ink beneath the skin.

As the city evolved, so did Joey's awareness. He saw that loyalty extended beyond personal ties it was also cultural. It meant loyalty to identity, to heritage, to community pride. To betray that was to forget where you came from. That idea became the cornerstone of his personality: no matter how far he went, he would never deny the streets that made him.

Years later, when the world would know his name for entirely different reasons, those early lessons would echo in every decision he made. The loyalty he learned in childhood fierce, protective, unyielding would drive both his triumphs and his struggles. It would be his compass and his chain, guiding him toward greatness and, at times, holding him to the weight of expectations no one could escape.

But in those early years, none of that mattered. What mattered was the unspoken bond between people who stood together, the comfort of a handshake that needed no contract, the quiet satisfaction of being trusted completely. Those moments built the foundation of who Joey Merlino was a young man learning that loyalty was not about obedience, but about honor.

He didn't yet know how far those lessons would take him or how much they would cost, but he knew one thing with certainty: in his world, loyalty wasn't optional. It was survival.

Chapter 3

The Making of "Skinny Joey"

The nickname came first, long before the reputation. In South Philadelphia, nicknames were a birthright. They carried stories, humor, and a sense of belonging. For Joey Merlino, the one that stuck "Skinny Joey" wasn't just a comment on his lean frame; it became the symbol of a new identity, one that walked the line between respect and rebellion.

He had grown into his confidence like a second skin. The restless energy of childhood had matured into something more controlled, more deliberate. By his late teens, Joey's posture had changed; his shoulders carried a quiet assurance, and his eyes missed little. He walked quickly, spoke decisively, and smiled often but the smile always carried intention. Every word, every gesture, every silence felt measured.

Around him, South Philly was shifting. The neighborhood's familiar rhythm the hum of corner cafés, the sound of radios spilling out Sinatra and Springsteen, the scent of espresso mingled with rain on asphalt masked the unease of economic change. Factories had closed, and opportunity grew scarce. For ambitious young men, the path forward often wound through small favors, quiet deals, and unspoken hierarchies.

Joey saw opportunity in the spaces between those lines. Where others saw limits, he saw negotiation. His natural charisma drew people in shop owners, mechanics, delivery drivers, older men who respected confidence when they saw it. They trusted him to handle errands, to keep track of who owed what, to remember details that others forgot. It wasn't power, not yet, but it was influence.

His friends began to notice how effortlessly he commanded attention. If a disagreement broke out, Joey stepped in. His words cut tension without humiliation. He had the instinct to know when to push and when to let someone save face. It made him likable, but also quietly intimidating. People realized that crossing him meant losing more than an argument; it meant losing access to his favor, his protection, and his respect.

The streets noticed.

Every neighborhood has its informal hierarchy men who run things, men who follow, and men who watch. Joey never declared his position, but everyone could see where he was headed. The older generation regarded him with a mix of pride and caution. He had inherited his father's discipline but wrapped it in youth's daring. There was a spark about him, the kind that could either illuminate or burn.

He learned to listen more than he spoke. That was his advantage. In cafés and pool halls, he absorbed stories from men twice his age stories about loyalty, silence, and what happened when either was broken. He didn't imitate them; he studied them. Each gesture, each pause, each coded phrase became part of his unspoken education.

By his early twenties, Joey's image had become a neighborhood signature. Sharp dresser, quick talker, confident to the edge of audacity. He could walk into a crowded room and immediately become its center, not by shouting but by commanding attention through presence alone. It wasn't arrogance; it was timing. He knew when to joke, when to flatter, and when to stare someone down until they looked away.

People called him "Skinny Joey" with affection, but behind the nickname was recognition. He had become someone who mattered. He was still young, but the streets treated him as an equal a man capable of both charm and consequence.

Still, ambition is a double-edged gift. Joey's hunger for independence, for recognition on his own terms, began to shape every decision. He wanted to build something lasting, something that couldn't be dismissed as his father's shadow. In a community where reputation was currency, he was determined to earn his own.

He began to surround himself with a tight circle of friends who shared his drive. They trusted each other completely. Their loyalty wasn't based on fear, but on years of friendship and shared history. They moved as one at parties, at local games, in the bars that dotted Passyunk Avenue. To outsiders, they looked like any group of confident young men chasing excitement. To those who knew better, they looked like the next generation of leadership taking shape quietly, naturally, inevitably.

Joey's ability to balance seriousness with humor became his most dangerous strength. He could make someone laugh right after delivering a warning. He could charm a critic into silence. His confidence, though magnetic, was rooted in discipline. He rose early, stayed alert, and never allowed excess to dull his focus. That restraint, rare among young men of his age, set him apart.

He also understood optics the quiet art of perception. He dressed sharply but never gaudily, choosing tailored suits that suggested respect rather than ostentation. When he entered a restaurant, he greeted staff by name. When someone owed him a favor, he never reminded them; he simply remembered. People began to talk about how he carried himself, how he seemed destined for something larger.

But destiny, as Joey would learn, always comes with tension.

The same qualities that made him admired also made him a target. Rivalries emerged, some subtle, others open. Older men who had grown comfortable in their positions saw him as both a successor and a threat. He wasn't seeking confrontation, but his very confidence created it. South Philly was a place where power was inherited slowly, not seized quickly and Joey's rise felt too fast, too visible.

There were whispers comparisons, predictions, warnings. He ignored them. For Joey, success wasn't about climbing over others; it was about mastering himself. Every challenge became a test of composure. He learned to let rumors roll off, to respond with calm defiance rather than anger. That restraint became legend. People might gossip, but no one could claim to have seen him lose control.

At night, when the streets quieted and the hum of conversation faded, Joey often walked alone. He liked the solitude, the rhythm of his footsteps echoing against the rowhouses. He thought about the choices that shaped men how one decision could build a lifetime of loyalty or erase it in a second. Those walks gave him perspective. They reminded him that charm could open doors, but only integrity kept them open.

He began to see leadership differently. It wasn't about power; it was about steadiness. People followed those they trusted to stay calm when everything else fell apart. That understanding became his foundation. He didn't seek admiration it came naturally. What he valued more was credibility.

As his name spread beyond his immediate neighborhood, Joey noticed the shift. People he had never met greeted him with deference. Shopkeepers offered him coffee before he ordered. Men from other parts of the city asked his opinion on disputes. He had become a symbol of youth, confidence, and a new era rising quietly beneath the old one.

But symbols are heavy things to carry. Every compliment added pressure. Every handshake carried expectation. The world around him began to read meanings into his actions that he hadn't spoken. Some saw him as a hero, others as a threat. In both cases, he became larger than himself "Skinny Joey," the image, the myth, the embodiment of South Philadelphia's grit and glamour.

His friends saw the toll it took. Behind the laughter and the effortless charm, Joey was always calculating, always watching. He trusted few outside his circle and relied on instinct when logic failed. Yet even in moments of uncertainty, he never lost that magnetic calm.

There were nights when he gathered his closest friends at small diners, away from the noise, and talked about loyalty not as a slogan, but as a philosophy. He told them that loyalty meant telling the truth, even when it hurt. It meant keeping your word when it was inconvenient. It meant standing by someone when everyone else walked away. Those conversations, quiet and private, revealed the man beneath the nickname thoughtful, disciplined, deeply aware of how fragile trust could be.

Joey's rise wasn't marked by grand gestures or public declarations. It was written in subtler ways in how he carried himself, in how others began to mirror his confidence. Young men in the neighborhood started to emulate his style: the crisp shirts, the quiet assertiveness, the refusal to be intimidated. He had become a blueprint for ambition.

Yet he never mistook admiration for friendship. He knew that the same crowd that cheered success could turn cold when times changed. His father had taught him that reputation could vanish overnight if built on ego instead of principle. Joey never forgot that. It kept him grounded, even as whispers of his influence spread.

In time, "Skinny Joey" became more than a name it became a paradox. To some, he was a gentleman, always respectful and generous. To others, he was a storm waiting for the right wind. What united both perspectives was fascination. Everyone, friend or critic, seemed drawn to the story of a young man who walked into every room as if he belonged there and somehow, he did.

Through it all, he remained loyal to his roots. He still visited the same cafés, greeted old neighbors, attended local events. Fame hadn't hardened him yet. He understood that the moment he forgot where he came from, he would lose everything that made him who he was.

Looking back, those years formed the heart of Joey Merlino's legend. They were the years when he turned from a restless boy into a man defined by charisma and control. Every smile, every measured silence, every firm handshake was a step toward the image that would later captivate both supporters and skeptics alike.

He didn't plan it that way. He simply lived by the rules that South Philadelphia had etched into him respect, loyalty, and composure. In a world that measured strength by noise, he proved that quiet confidence could be just as commanding.

As the decade turned and the city changed again, "Skinny Joey" would find himself standing at the edge of a new chapter one that would test everything he believed about loyalty, ambition, and survival. But in these early years, before fame, before controversy, before the weight of public attention, he was something purer: a young man determined to define himself on his own terms, guided by instinct, strengthened by loyalty, and driven by a hunger to matter.

Chapter 4

Blood and Power

The streets of Philadelphia were changing again, and this time the transformation came not from the slow creep of industry or culture, but from within. Beneath the familiar rhythm of neighborhood life the sound of car horns on Broad Street, the aroma of espresso spilling from corner cafés, the chatter of people who knew one another by name an invisible tension began to hum. It was the sound of an empire shifting.

The early 1990s were years of uncertainty for South Philadelphia. Old loyalties were crumbling, and new alliances were being tested by ambition, fear, and survival. The once-unshakable foundations of the local underworld had weakened after decades of internal conflict and federal attention. Into this uneasy silence, a new generation began to rise bold, restless, unwilling to live under old rules that no longer fit the times. At the center of that storm stood Joey Merlino.

By now, "Skinny Joey" was no longer just a neighborhood name whispered with curiosity or admiration. He had become a symbol to some, of rebellion against outdated leadership; to others, a sign of everything reckless about youth in a world built on patience. His confidence, once admired, now carried consequence. His popularity drew loyalty, but also danger. In a city where power had always been handed down carefully, Joey's ascent felt like a revolution.

To understand what came next, one had to understand the moment he stepped into. The 1990s were not kind to the old guard. Leadership had fractured, and men once bound by loyalty had begun to suspect each other's motives. The name *John Stanfa* had become synonymous with both control and controversy. Older, traditional, and deeply protective of the past, Stanfa represented the old order the final breath of a generation that had survived its prime.

Joey, by contrast, embodied the future sharp, modern, unapologetically bold. He was everything the new decade demanded: adaptive, media-aware, and willing to lead from the front rather than from shadows. The collision between those two worlds was inevitable.

For months, whispers grew. Meetings that once ended with handshakes now ended with silence. Friends became cautious. The air in South Philly cafés grew thicker, conversations shorter. Even those who had nothing to do with the conflict could feel it. It was a neighborhood instinct the subtle awareness that something was about to give way.

Through it all, Joey carried himself with characteristic calm. He wasn't naïve; he understood the stakes. But unlike many, he didn't believe fear was the way to maintain control. He believed respect had to be earned, not demanded. To him, leadership wasn't about hierarchy; it was about trust and consistency. People followed him because they wanted to, not because they were told to.

That belief made him dangerous to those who built their power on tradition.

As tension mounted, alliances began to form quietly around Joey. Young men, many of whom had grown up alongside him, saw in him something rare a sense of direction amid chaos. They admired his clarity, his refusal to hide behind others, his unwavering loyalty to those who stood with him. He wasn't simply fighting for influence; he was fighting for a new way of leading.

But every rise invites resistance.

The conflict that unfolded in Philadelphia during those years was not a story of greed alone it was a story of identity. It was about who would define what loyalty meant in a changing world. For decades, leadership had meant obedience. Now, it began to mean initiative. Joey's defiance was not reckless; it was philosophical. He didn't seek to destroy the old order he sought to rebuild it on different terms.

Still, change never comes peacefully.

The streets, once alive with the hum of everyday life, became fields of quiet suspicion. Car windows stayed up longer. Strangers lingered less. The laughter that once echoed from cafés carried an edge of unease. Even the most ordinary nights felt heavy with potential.

To Joey, it was both exhilarating and sobering. He had wanted independence, but now independence carried the weight of responsibility. Every move mattered. Every word could shift the balance of trust. The young leader who had once disarmed tension with charm now had to navigate a world where a smile could be misread as challenge.

Through it all, his circle remained tight bound by years of friendship and mutual faith. They were young, but not naïve. They knew what loyalty demanded. They stood together not because they shared ambition, but because they shared belief. It was them against uncertainty, and that bond gave them strength.

Meanwhile, across the city, the old guard watched. They had built their lives on rules carved in stone, and Joey represented something they couldn't control movement, adaptation, change. His refusal to bow to tradition infuriated them. They mistook his confidence for arrogance, his vision for recklessness.

It was inevitable that these two worlds would collide.

When they finally did, it wasn't in a single explosion but a slow unraveling a test of endurance, loyalty, and nerve. The tension spilled from whispers to headlines, from shadows to daylight. The city that had once treated such matters with quiet discretion now found itself reading names in newspapers, seeing faces on screens. Philadelphia's streets, once bound by silence, had become an open stage.

Joey understood the danger of visibility, but he also understood its power. If the world was going to watch, he decided, he would control the narrative. He projected composure, even charm, when others expected fear. That balance of confidence under pressure became his defining feature. It made him unpredictable and, paradoxically, respected.

But leadership in times of turmoil comes at a price. Behind the poise, the long nights grew heavier. Decisions that once came easily now carried weight. Every choice could save one person but endanger another. Every friendship could become a liability. The cost of power was no longer abstract it was personal.

Those who knew Joey best said he changed during those years. Not outwardly he still laughed easily, still carried that quiet swagger but his eyes told a different story. They held calculation, fatigue, reflection. He had learned that being feared was simpler than being respected, but far less rewarding.

As the conflict deepened, the old order began to fracture. Trust eroded from within. Some men sought protection, others fled, and some simply vanished from the landscape of influence altogether. The city's balance shifted. The era of John Stanfa's authority waned under the weight of its own rigidity.

And out of that decline, Joey's rise became undeniable.

He didn't take control through spectacle; he earned it through endurance. When others retreated, he remained. When others doubted, he acted. He became the figure people looked to not because he demanded loyalty, but because he embodied it. In a world built on silence, his steadiness spoke louder than any threat.

For the first time, the name Joey Merlino carried not just recognition it carried inevitability. To those who followed him, he represented survival in a world that had forgotten how to evolve. To those who opposed him, he represented the loss of everything they once controlled.

Philadelphia was no stranger to change, but this was different. This was generational. It was not merely about crime or power; it was about identity who would carry forward the traditions of loyalty, community, and control into a new century that no longer respected the old rules.

And at the heart of it, a man who understood both worlds raised in the shadow of the past, but unwilling to live within it.

The transformation of Joey Merlino from neighborhood son to central figure in Philadelphia's shifting hierarchy was not the product of violence, though violence surrounded it. It was the product of conviction a belief that leadership had to evolve or vanish. His version of power was rooted in presence, not domination. People gravitated toward him because he made them feel part of something that mattered, something that still honored the word "loyalty," even as the world around them changed.

Still, the cost of that power was steep. The same charisma that drew people close also drew scrutiny. His every move, every friendship, every public appearance became a subject of analysis. The city he once ruled with silence now watched him with fascination and judgment.

Through all of it, Joey remained composed. He spoke rarely, but when he did, his words carried weight. He reminded those around him that respect was not given it was built, tested, and proven. His leadership, for all its controversy, was rooted in something unshakable: the belief that power without honor was hollow.

By the mid-1990s, Philadelphia had changed again. The names that once defined its underworld had faded. The rules that once governed its streets had been rewritten. In their place stood a man who refused to be a relic of the past or a victim of the future. Joey Merlino had become the face of a new era an era where strength was measured not just by control, but by resilience.

The city, weary of chaos yet addicted to its mythology, found in him a paradox: the leader it couldn't decide whether to fear or admire. And as the decade moved forward, his story would transcend the streets entirely moving into courtrooms, headlines, and the public imagination.

But in these turbulent years, amid betrayal and survival, Joey learned the hardest truth of all that every act of loyalty eventually demands a test. Power could be taken, lost, rebuilt, but loyalty could never be forced. It had to be chosen, and it could vanish in a heartbeat.

For all the titles and nicknames the world would later assign him, it was this understanding earned through conflict, loss, and endurance that defined who he truly was.

The boy from South Philadelphia, once known simply as "Skinny Joey," had become something far larger than his name. He was no longer just a son of the neighborhood; he was its reflection flawed, proud, relentless, and unwilling to surrender to anyone's version of his destiny but his own.

Chapter 5

The Celebrity Mobster

By the mid-1990s, Philadelphia had become the stage for a drama unlike any other in America's criminal landscape. The old codes of silence that once governed the streets were being rewritten, not by violence alone, but by visibility. And standing in the center of it all smiling for cameras, shaking hands with reporters, and turning every court appearance into a photo opportunity was Joey Merlino, the man the media would crown "the celebrity mobster."

To understand the magnetism that surrounded Joey, one had to look beyond the headlines. His presence wasn't merely newsworthy it was cinematic. The city had seen gangsters before, men who operated from the shadows, speaking only through whispers or coded gestures. Joey broke that mold completely. He was polished, confident, and charismatic, moving through Philadelphia like a man born for attention. Dressed in sharp suits that caught the light, he carried himself with an ease that disarmed people. He could walk into a courtroom and look like he was entering a dinner party. Even the federal agents watching him from across the street couldn't help but admit he had style.

To the people in South Philly, Joey wasn't just a headline; he was their guy. He attended neighborhood events, donated to local charities, and handed out toys to children during the holidays. For a city that often felt forgotten by the political elite, Joey represented something familiar a man who never left the block he grew up on. His charm was real, but it was also strategic. He understood that being liked gave him protection in ways that fear could not. When people adored you, they defended you. And Joey Merlino, more than anyone, understood the value of loyalty dressed as affection.

But not everyone saw his charm as harmless. To law enforcement, his confidence was arrogance, his openness a challenge. The FBI watched as he turned every public appearance into a performance. They saw a man who seemed untouchable who laughed on his way into the courthouse and smiled as he walked out, even when facing serious charges. In an era when the Mafia was supposed to be fading into obscurity, Joey was rewriting the rules. He wasn't hiding in back rooms; he was sitting in front-row seats at sporting events, being photographed at clubs, and dining in restaurants where reporters could find him. He had turned himself into a paradox a man accused of being a mob boss who behaved like a movie star.

That transformation didn't happen by accident. Joey had always understood image as power. He once told an acquaintance that if people were going to talk about him, they might as well talk about something worth hearing. It wasn't ego it was strategy. Every story about him in the press gave him control over the narrative, even when it wasn't flattering. He learned that fame, even infamy, could be a shield. The brighter the spotlight, the harder it was for his enemies to move in the dark.

As newspapers splashed his name across their front pages, Joey became an unexpected celebrity. Journalists compared him to the fictional mobsters who had captured the public imagination. His photo was printed beside stories about famous actors and sports figures. Nightly news segments described him with a strange fascination half warning, half admiration. To some, he was a throwback to an older time, when gangsters had manners and style. To others, he was the symbol of a new kind of underworld one that blended crime with charisma.

His public appearances became legendary. Outside the federal courthouse, crowds would gather not just out of curiosity, but out of loyalty. Some cheered as he walked by, others asked for autographs. Even those who had never met him spoke of him with a kind of fond disbelief as if he were part of the city's folklore. Joey didn't run from the attention; he thrived on it. When asked about his notoriety, he once smiled and said, "If they're talking, that means they're watching." It was a simple truth and a dangerous one.

Inside the justice system, his image worked against him. Prosecutors painted him as the ringleader of a violent enterprise, using his public confidence as proof of arrogance. Every smile, every quote, every headline became ammunition in court. Yet even as they built their cases, they couldn't deny his influence. Joey had become something more than a defendant he was a phenomenon. Reporters described his courtroom as if it were a red-carpet event, with cameras flashing and crowds murmuring as he entered. He seemed unbothered by it all, greeting his lawyers like old friends, waving at the familiar faces in the crowd. He wasn't just fighting charges; he was performing a role he had crafted perfectly that of the untouchable man.

For Joey, the attention wasn't just about vanity. It was about control. In a world where stories could destroy a man, he made sure his story was told on his terms. He granted interviews sparingly but strategically, speaking with just enough charm to intrigue the public without ever revealing too much. Every gesture was measured every word, chosen carefully. He walked a thin line between fascination and danger, between reality and myth. And for a while, it worked beautifully.

Television networks loved him. He was unpredictable, articulate, and unapologetic the kind of character that made audiences tune in. Magazine profiles painted him as a "modern outlaw," someone who mixed old-school charm with new-world media savvy. Even the fashion choices that once seemed vain became part of his identity. The suits, the shoes, the ever-present tan all became symbols of who he was: a man who refused to fade into the background.

But behind the glamour and the grin was a man constantly calculating. Joey knew that every headline carried a cost. The cameras that adored him could also condemn him. Law enforcement agencies doubled their efforts, convinced that anyone so comfortable in the spotlight must have something to hide. Surveillance increased. Informants multiplied. Every move he made, every handshake, every smile was recorded, analyzed, and reported. Yet Joey continued, almost defiantly, as if proving that charm could be a weapon sharper than fear.

For the younger generation in Philadelphia, Joey represented something rare a man who made the city feel alive again. While others saw chaos, they saw charisma. He had turned South Philly into a legend once more, a place where stories were told in whispers and laughter, not fear. To them, Joey was living proof that you could come from their streets and become somebody the whole country talked about. They overlooked the danger because they were drawn to the dream the idea that confidence could be power, and power could be beautiful.

Still, fame is a fragile currency. As the years passed, the weight of Joey's image began to press against him. Every new headline brought new scrutiny. Every act of generosity was questioned, every word dissected. The same charm that had lifted him up now began to draw suspicion. People wondered where the act ended and the man began. Was Joey truly the good-natured neighborhood figure he appeared to be, or was that image another layer of the game?

Yet even in the midst of doubt, one thing remained undeniable: Joey Merlino had changed the rules. He had taken a life built on secrecy and turned it into a spectacle. The old guard called him reckless; the young called him brilliant. And while others faded into history, Joey's name continued to echo. He wasn't just another figure in the underworld he had become part of American culture, an unlikely celebrity who blurred the line between danger and entertainment.

The press couldn't get enough of him. They followed him to restaurants, snapped photos of him shopping, even speculated on his personal life. He was discussed on radio shows and late-night television, turning court dates into episodes of ongoing drama. It was as if Philadelphia itself had become addicted to the story and Joey, ever the showman, gave them something new every time. He never ranted or raged; he smiled. Even when accused, even when challenged, he remained calm, almost amused, as if he knew something no one else did.

And perhaps he did. Joey understood that the modern world ran on attention and attention could make a man powerful in ways money never could. Long before social media made it common to live publicly, he was already doing it instinctively. He had turned perception into armor, making his myth so large that it was impossible to destroy completely. Even when his name was dragged through headlines, it stayed there alive, undeniable.

Through it all, the essence of Joey Merlino remained consistent. He was bold, unpredictable, and unwaveringly loyal to his image. He gave people something to believe in whether it was real or not didn't seem to matter. His world was one where stories became currency, and he spent his carefully. He understood better than most that legends aren't created by truth alone, but by how well one lives the story others want to tell.

By the time the decade closed, Joey was no longer just a man; he was an idea a reflection of how fame could transform even the darkest reputations into fascination. The media had crowned him, the public had embraced him, and the system had tried to break him. Yet through every charge, every headline, and every photograph, he remained exactly what he had always been a man unafraid to live in the open.

The world had given him a label "the celebrity mobster." Joey Merlino had accepted it, reshaped it, and owned it completely. And in doing so, he ensured that his story would never be forgotten.

Chapter 6

Love, Family, and the Life

For all the noise that surrounded Joey Merlino, there was another world quieter, more intimate, and hidden from the flashing lights. Behind the headlines, beneath the surface of courtroom stories and front-page photos, lived a man who tried, however imperfectly, to balance two opposing worlds: the family he loved and the life that defined him.

The public saw Joey as the confident, smiling figure in tailored suits the man who shook hands with neighbors, traded jokes with reporters, and turned every encounter into a story. But at home, in the rare moments when the noise faded and the cameras disappeared, he was simply Joey a husband, a father, and a man fighting to keep his two lives from colliding.

Love, for him, wasn't simple. It never could be for someone raised in a world where loyalty and secrecy governed every breath. To love someone deeply meant exposing them to risk; to keep them safe often meant keeping them in the dark. That paradox haunted Joey's private life from the very beginning.

When he married Deborah, he wasn't the "celebrity mobstcr" thc world would later know he was still a young man trying to find balance between ambition and affection. Deborah wasn't drawn to the image the media later built around him. She knew the man beneath it the one who could be unexpectedly gentle, who listened, who cared deeply about family and appearances, who carried a pride that sometimes looked like defiance but often came from a need to protect those closest to him.

Their marriage, like the city they called home, was built on a mix of toughness and tenderness. South Philadelphia wasn't a place for the faint of heart. Families there grew close because the world outside demanded it. Privacy wasn't just a preference; it was protection. Within those narrow row houses and tight-knit communities, everyone knew someone who lived between two realities the family dinner table and the unspoken world that existed beyond it. Joey's home was no different.

Inside, Deborah created a world of normalcy. The clatter of dinner plates, the hum of evening television, the laughter of children these were her ways of grounding a life that could so easily spin out of control. Joey adored his daughters. He would light up when talking about them, his eyes softening in a way they never did in public. He might have lived with constant pressure outside, but when he was home, he was a father before anything else. He played with them, teased them, and protected them fiercely.

Yet love couldn't erase the shadow that followed him. Every phone call, every knock at the door, every whisper carried the weight of his other life. Deborah knew that being with Joey meant living with uncertainty the late-night calls, the sudden trips, the endless scrutiny from law enforcement. But she also knew the other side the loyalty, the humor, the deep sense of family that had always been part of him.

Joey's world was built on two definitions of loyalty one born of love, the other of the life. To outsiders, they seemed the same, but inside, he knew how different they truly were. The loyalty of "the life" demanded silence, secrecy, and sacrifice. The loyalty of family demanded honesty, openness, and care. He was caught between them, trying to honor both but always at risk of losing one.

Still, Joey believed that family made him stronger. He would often say that having something to lose gave a man reason to fight harder. When he was home, he wasn't the man in the headlines; he was just Joey fixing a lightbulb, laughing over coffee, talking about the future. It was in those moments that his charm felt most real, stripped of performance.

For Deborah, love became a form of endurance. She stood by him through every trial, every rumor, every article that twisted their lives into entertainment. She learned to smile when she wanted to scream, to hold her family together when the world tried to pull it apart. She raised their children with grace, determined that they would know their father not through headlines but through the quiet acts of love he showed them the bedtime stories, the hugs before school, the laughter that filled the kitchen.

Even as the pressure mounted the investigations, the accusations, the relentless media coverage Joey held on to that domestic world. He made time for birthdays and holidays, even when court appearances loomed. He took his daughters to the beach, to ball games, to dinner. Those were the moments he lived for the simple, fleeting seconds when he could forget the cameras, the whispers, the constant watchfulness.

But the outside world never truly left him. The life had a way of seeping into everything, even the quietest corners. Sometimes it arrived in the form of an unexpected visitor; other times, in a phone call that changed the mood of the entire evening. Deborah learned to read his expressions the way his jaw would tighten, the way his tone would shift. She didn't always ask questions; some answers were better left unspoken.

Still, she loved him not the myth, but the man. She loved the way he carried himself, the way he fought for those he cared about, the way he refused to bow to pressure. And he, in turn, loved her strength. He often said she was tougher than most men he'd known, and in many ways, she was. It took resilience to live beside Joey Merlino resilience, patience, and faith.

In quiet moments, Joey sometimes wondered what his life might have been if he'd chosen another path if he'd been a businessman, or a coach, or simply another South Philly guy who grew up and moved on. But reflection didn't suit him for long. He was who he was, shaped by the streets, by family, by the unspoken rules of the world he'd inherited. The best he could do was protect what he loved, even if he couldn't always shield it from the consequences of his choices.

Fatherhood changed him more than anything else. Holding his daughters, watching them grow, made him realize how fragile everything truly was. He wanted better for them not wealth, not fame, but peace. The kind of peace he'd never known. He taught them respect, manners, and pride in where they came from, but he also taught them to stay away from the life that had defined his own. He wanted them to see the world beyond Philadelphia's narrow blocks, to dream without fear.

Those who knew Joey privately often said that he was a different man with his family softer, protective, patient in ways that surprised them. The same man who could stare down a rival with unflinching confidence could also kneel to tie his daughter's shoe or spend hours helping with homework. It was in those moments that the contradictions of his life were clearest the man of loyalty and love, of danger and tenderness, existing side by side.

Yet even love couldn't rewrite history. There were nights when Deborah sat awake long after he'd gone to bed, wondering what future awaited them. The world outside was unpredictable. There were always eyes watching, always questions whispered. But she stayed not out of denial, but out of devotion. She believed in the man behind the myth, and that belief became the foundation of their family.

As years passed and the spotlight intensified, Joey tried to shield his home from it. Reporters camped near their neighborhood, tabloids speculated endlessly, and federal agents never truly disappeared. But inside the house, life continued. Dinner was served, laughter echoed through the rooms, and photographs lined the walls not of power or fame, but of birthdays, holidays, and simple, ordinary moments.

Through all of it, Joey's guiding principle remained the same: family first. He had learned that from his own father, and despite their complicated past, he carried that lesson forward. Loyalty to family wasn't just a word; it was a duty. It meant being present, being protective, and being willing to bear the weight of the world if it meant keeping them safe.

And so, even when the headlines grew darker, even when the trials returned and the world speculated endlessly about his life, Joey held on to that one unshakable truth. His name might belong to the streets, but his heart belonged to his home.

For all the charm and confidence that made him a public fascination, it was love not power that grounded him. It was Deborah's steadiness, his daughters' laughter, the smell of dinner cooking in a small Philadelphia kitchen that gave him something real to hold onto. The world could take his freedom, his reputation, even his peace of mind. But it could never take that.

Because for Joey Merlino, no matter what the world believed, family was the only empire that truly mattered.

Chapter 7

The Party Never Ends

For most men, the storm of federal investigations, newspaper scandals, and courtroom drama would have been enough to drive them underground. But Joey Merlino was not most men. Where others saw danger, he saw opportunity. Where others hid, he stepped into the light confident, stylish, and completely at ease under the gaze of a city that couldn't stop talking about him.

By the late 1990s, as Philadelphia's underworld simmered and law enforcement hovered on every corner, Joey's social calendar looked more like that of a rising celebrity than that of a man under constant surveillance. Clubs, charity dinners, fundraisers if there was an event worth attending, Joey was there, his presence as magnetic as ever. It wasn't arrogance that drew him in; it was something deeper, almost instinctive. He believed that to survive in a world obsessed with stories, you had to be seen. You had to own the narrative before someone else wrote it for you.

And so, he did.

On any given night, he could be found at one of Philadelphia's upscale lounges not hiding in a corner, but greeting people at the door. The music would pulse low through the dimly lit rooms, laughter spilling out into the street, and there he would be: "Skinny Joey", dressed immaculately in a tailored suit, a gold watch flashing as he shook hands, offered smiles, and lifted a glass in toast. He wasn't just attending parties he was hosting them, commanding them. Even those who didn't dare approach couldn't help but watch.

His charisma made people forget the tension that followed him. They saw only the man who knew how to make a room feel alive. He laughed easily, complimented freely, and never stayed in one place too long just long enough to leave an impression. To outsiders, it seemed effortless; to those who knew him well, it was all part of the performance. Joey had learned long ago that appearances were a kind of power. Every smile was a signal, every gesture a message.

But his nights out weren't just about glamour they were also about strategy. The city's elite often mingled in the same places as its hustlers, and Joey navigated both worlds with ease. He could talk business with a lawyer, crack jokes with a bartender, and charm a local politician all in the span of a single evening. He understood people what they wanted, what they feared, and most importantly, how they wanted to be seen in his presence. For many, being associated with Joey added a kind of intrigue, a thrill. He was dangerous, but polite; unpredictable, but magnetic.

Those who saw him at charity events often came away surprised. They expected intimidation, but found generosity. Joey gave openly to causes that mattered to him children's programs, community drives, neighborhood fundraisers. He wasn't shy about it either. He showed up in person, not as a benefactor behind the scenes, but as a participant. He mingled with volunteers, shook hands with organizers, and made sure that every person he met remembered him as more than the man in the headlines.

The paradox fascinated people. Here was a man accused of leading an underworld empire, standing on stage at a gala, bidding on silent auction items, smiling for photos beside local officials. It was surreal almost cinematic. Some whispered that it was all a show, an attempt to polish his image. Others said it was genuine, that Joey had always been the kind of man who gave back to the community that raised him. The truth, as always, lived somewhere in between.

He had a talent for making chaos look like charm. While others in his world struggled to stay unseen, Joey seemed to thrive on visibility. The more he appeared in public, the more untouchable he seemed. To his supporters, it was a sign of confidence proof that he had nothing to hide. To his detractors, it was arrogance a man tempting fate. But Joey didn't care what they thought. The way he saw it, the city would always talk. Better they talk about his generosity and style than about things whispered in backrooms.

He lived by a rhythm few could match. Mornings might bring meetings with lawyers or quiet breakfasts with family, but by nightfall, he was often back in motion a fixture at the heart of Philadelphia's social scene. Whether it was a charity dinner or a nightclub opening, his arrival changed the atmosphere. Cameras flashed, conversations paused, heads turned. He didn't need to announce himself; his presence did that for him.

To those who watched closely, though, there was a subtle tension beneath the polish. Every outing carried risk. Every appearance was a dance between visibility and vulnerability. There were nights when plainclothes agents watched from across the room, their eyes hidden behind the glow of cocktail glasses. Joey knew they were there; sometimes he even acknowledged them with a nod or a smirk. He understood the game he'd been playing it his whole life.

In truth, the parties were his escape. They were a way to breathe amid the constant pressure. Music and laughter drowned out the hum of suspicion. In those moments, surrounded by people who adored him, Joey could almost forget that he lived under a microscope. The rhythm of the night offered him something courtrooms never could freedom, even if only for a few hours.

People often described him as having an aura something beyond charm. It was presence, confidence, a kind of warmth that made people feel seen, even if only briefly. Women admired him, men respected him, and everyone wanted to understand him. Yet Joey remained just out of reach, his true thoughts hidden behind that trademark half-smile. He could make you feel like you knew him, but you never really did.

One evening at a charity banquet downtown, a reporter asked him what he thought about his "celebrity" status. Joey had just finished bidding on a children's hospital donation package. He paused, smiled lightly, and said, "You can't buy respect but you can earn it, even when they don't want to give it." Then he walked away, leaving the room to interpret his words however they pleased. It was pure Merlino confident, cryptic, and controlled.

What few realized was how carefully he maintained that balance between light and shadow. Every public appearance was calculated, every gesture rehearsed. He knew when to leave, when to linger, when to let the cameras catch his smile and when to walk away. He was a master of timing, both on the streets and in the spotlight.

Behind the scenes, Deborah often worried. She understood the appeal, but she also saw the danger. The more Joey mingled with the public, the more he invited scrutiny. Every photograph could become evidence, every rumor could spark investigation. Yet trying to change him was impossible. Joey wasn't built to hide. He believed that showing strength even through celebration was part of survival. To him, disappearing would mean defeat.

Even his enemies couldn't deny his charm. Rival figures, law enforcement officers, even prosecutors admitted privately that he had a presence few could match. He could make a room of skeptics laugh, disarm suspicion with humor, and turn strangers into allies in minutes. It was that very quality that magnetism that made him so difficult to pin down. People wanted to believe in him, to see the good, the generous, the human behind the myth.

In time, Joey's nights out became as much a part of his identity as his reputation. He wasn't just known for the life he was known for the lifestyle. He blurred the lines so seamlessly that it became impossible to tell where the man ended and the image began. The parties weren't just celebrations; they were statements. Each one said, *I'm still here. I'm still standing.*

When the music faded and the lights dimmed, Joey would often step outside alone, the night air cool against his face. The city stretched around him the same streets he'd walked since childhood, now lit with the glow of a hundred flashing bulbs. For a moment, he would stand there quietly, taking it in the laughter spilling from doorways, the faint echo of his name whispered by strangers. Then, just as always, he'd smile that familiar, knowing smile and slip back into the crowd, as if he belonged to the night itself.

To some, Joey Merlino was a gangster who learned to act like a gentleman. To others, he was a gentleman who happened to be born into the wrong kind of world. But for those who truly understood him, he was something rarer still a man who refused to be defined by anyone but himself.

The party never really ended for Joey, because the party was never just about celebration. It was survival. It was presence. It was proof. In every laugh, every handshake, every spotlight that found his face, he was making a quiet declaration to the city that loved him and feared him in equal measure:

You can watch me. You can judge me. But you will never forget me.

Chapter 8

Trials, Tapes, and Betrayals

There was a time when Joey Merlino could walk into any restaurant in Philadelphia and command a room without saying a word. Heads turned, whispers rippled, and somewhere between admiration and fear, people made space for him. His reputation carried its own gravity. But by the late 1990s, that gravity began to shift. The air in South Philadelphia changed. Friends began watching each other with quiet suspicion. Unmarked cars appeared at odd corners. And in the background, the faint hum of a new kind of war one fought not with bullets, but with recorders, wiretaps, and deals.

The laughter that once echoed through Joey's favorite haunts began to sound different, thinner, like a party that had gone on too long. The nightclubs were still full, the champagne still cold, but the eyes at the tables no longer looked only at him they looked over their shoulders. It was the beginning of the end, though few recognized it then.

The Invisible Audience

The agents had been watching for months. What started as casual observation became an obsession inside the offices of the Federal Bureau of Investigation. Every move Joey made, every voice that reached his orbit, was tracked, logged, and dissected. They weren't after quick arrests; they were building a case that would pierce the myth of "Skinny Joey," the so-called modern-day gentleman of Philadelphia's underworld.

They planted ears in cars, offices, and corners of cafes that had once felt safe. They flipped associates men who had sworn loyalty in whispers now whispering to agents for promises of leniency or protection. No one could have known that even the faintest laugh, a coded phrase, or a passing comment could one day become the soundtrack of betrayal.

Joey still moved through the city as if untouchable tailored suits, gold cross gleaming at the neck, a calm swagger that told the world he wasn't afraid. But beneath that calm, something in him sensed the shift. The old codes of silence and loyalty were eroding, not by bullets, but by microphones and fear. What the old bosses never imagined was that the fall would not come from rivals but from technology from the very voices of the people closest to them.

Echoes on Tape

When the FBI finally began to reveal what they had gathered, it was staggering. Hours upon hours of conversations, coded exchanges, and offhand remarks that, when pieced together, painted a vivid picture of a world built on relationships, loyalty, and quiet authority. Some tapes caught Joey joking, others caught him frustrated. To prosecutors, each word was a thread. To Joey, they were just the sounds of everyday life but in the sterile silence of a courtroom, they became evidence.

There was no dramatic movie-style discovery, no single tape that ended everything. It was accumulation a slow tightening of rope. What was once rumor began to take shape in official reports. What had been friendship became testimony. The invisible web around him grew smaller each day.

Still, Joey held his composure. He laughed at headlines, appeared confident before the cameras, and insisted he was being targeted because of who people thought he was not because of what he did. It was a familiar refrain in Philadelphia, where the line between reputation and reality was always blurry. To the public, Joey remained the city's most fascinating paradox the man who smiled in the face of accusation.

The Betrayal Within

The betrayal didn't come from enemies. It came from inside from the same familiar faces that had shared toasts, jokes, and late-night drives. Some were frightened. Others felt cornered. And in the end, when the government offered safety or leniency, they accepted.

It was the kind of betrayal that cuts deeper than any rival's bullet the slow realization that trust had been traded for survival. Joey once said that loyalty was everything, the single rule that defined a man. Now, he was living in a world where loyalty had become a currency, and too many were willing to sell.

Inside the investigation, agents quietly celebrated each new defection. One name led to another. And with every insider who stepped forward, the once-solid foundation of Joey's circle began to crumble. But on the outside, Joey refused to bend. He didn't hide or vanish. He walked into restaurants, played golf, waved to the cameras. His defiance became a performance part pride, part denial, part instinct. It was as if he believed that by acting unafraid, he could keep the illusion alive.

But no performance lasts forever.

The Long Road to Trial

By the late 1990s, the storm had grown too large to ignore. Indictments were unsealed, headlines exploded, and the image of "Skinny Joey" once a figure of fascination was now framed under the harsh glare of federal charges. For months, the newspapers painted a picture of a man at war with both his enemies and the system. The coverage was relentless. Some stories speculated on alliances, others focused on fashion or attitude, as if charisma itself were a kind of evidence.

The courtroom became his stage. Cameras waited outside every morning, eager to capture that trademark grin. He wore it like armor, the same grin that once lit up nightclubs now turned toward the press confident, ironic, unbroken. Inside, though, the tension was electric. The stakes were no longer about image but about freedom.

Witnesses testified. Recordings played. Each word from the tapes echoed through the courtroom like the slow tick of a clock counting down a man's old life. Prosecutors tried to paint him as a leader; defense attorneys argued he was a target a name too famous to ignore. The trial dragged on for months, an exhausting spectacle that left the city divided between fascination and fatigue.

When the verdict finally came, the silence was heavier than any cheer or gasp. Joey stood tall, unflinching, as the words were read. The gavel fell, and history moved forward but the myth of "Skinny Joey" refused to die. Even in defeat, he seemed to win something intangible: the story.

Behind the Bars, Beyond the Headlines

Prison stripped away the glamour. There were no lights, no headlines, no tailored suits just the quiet rhythm of time and reflection. But even behind the bars, Joey found a way to adapt. Those who knew him during that time spoke of a man who refused bitterness. He exercised daily, read constantly, and wrote letters that mixed humor with hard truth. He didn't dwell on what he'd lost but on what he still had family, name, and faith.

Outside, the legend grew. Each story, each rumor, each whispered memory of Joey Merlino on the streets of South Philadelphia became part of a larger mythology. People spoke of him in the present tense even when he was gone from sight. His name still carried a strange electricity a mix of nostalgia and defiance.

In the end, that was Joey's true gift. He understood how people saw him, and he used it. Even from afar, he managed to stay relevant. His absence only made the fascination stronger.

The Price of the Spotlight

Looking back, it's clear that Joey's rise and fall weren't just about law or loyalty. They were about visibility the danger of living in a spotlight that never turns off. For decades, the unwritten rule of survival in that world was simple: stay quiet, stay invisible. Joey did the opposite. He was public, charismatic, unguarded. The cameras that once made him a star also made him a target.

He had rewritten the old codes without realizing how much that would cost. Every smile became a symbol. Every quote a headline. Every friendship a potential liability. The myth he built became a cage one that followed him long after the doors of prison opened again.

And yet, even knowing all that, Joey never expressed regret for being who he was. He had played his role fully, without disguise. "You live your life once," he once said in an interview years later. "Might as well live it your way." It wasn't arrogance it was philosophy. For a man raised on loyalty, pride, and resilience, it was his final defense.

The Aftermath of Betrayal

When Joey finally returned to the outside world, he walked into a city that had changed. Philadelphia was cleaner, quieter, more cautious. The old faces had scattered. Some had moved on. Others had disappeared altogether. The neighborhoods still whispered his name, but the tone had shifted from awe to memory.

The betrayals of the past still lingered, like echoes in familiar streets. Some of the people who once called him brother now crossed the street to avoid eye contact. But Joey didn't dwell on bitterness. He had learned something inside: holding onto anger only gives power to the past. Instead, he focused on rebuilding not the empire that once was, but the life that could still be.

He returned to his family, to faith, to a quieter rhythm. But the irony was that Joey could never truly disappear. Even when he tried to live simply, to open a restaurant or keep his head down, the world refused to forget. Reporters still called. Cameras still showed up. Every move still made news. The fascination had outlived the reason for it.

And so he lived between two worlds the private man who wanted peace and the public legend who refused to fade.

A City That Never Forgot

Philadelphia has a way of remembering its own, especially the ones who break its rules while somehow embodying its spirit. Joey was one of those rare figures who belonged to the city as much as he defined it. The old-timers still told stories about his father, the next generation spoke of Joey like a ghost the man who once made the streets buzz with life and danger and excitement.

The younger crowd, who knew him only through documentaries and news clips, saw something else a symbol of rebellion, charm, and endurance. To them, he wasn't just a man; he was a character from a story that refused to end. The lines between truth and legend blurred long ago. What mattered now was that his name still carried weight, a reminder of a time when loyalty was a way of life and betrayal was the only unforgivable sin.

The Lesson Beneath the Noise

If there was a lesson buried beneath the years of trials, betrayals, and headlines, it was this: power built on fear crumbles, but power built on identity lasts. Joey had lost much friends, freedom, privacy yet he never lost himself. Even at his lowest, he remained unmistakably him: bold, proud, composed, human.

And perhaps that's why his story endures. Because it isn't just about one man against the law. It's about what happens when a person refuses to be defined by the world's version of him. It's about the fine line between fame and infamy, between leadership and downfall, between loyalty and survival.

In the quiet moments after it all after the trials, after the tapes, after the betrayals Joey Merlino stood as proof that even when the empire falls, the legend endures.

The watchers may have recorded every word. The prosecutors may have taken years of his life. But what they could never capture was the essence of what made him who he was a man shaped by loyalty, undone by betrayal, and still somehow standing in the light when the dust settled.

Even now, the sound of those tapes the ones that once threatened to destroy him feels like an echo of something larger. They are reminders that every world built on trust is fragile, every code is tested, and every story has two sides.

And in Joey's case, both sides the man and the myth still breathe in the same body.

Chapter 9

Behind Bars and Beyond

When the steel doors closed behind Joey Merlino, the noise of the outside world faded into silence. For years, he had lived in the hum of attention the flash of cameras, the rhythm of headlines, the restless pulse of city streets that seemed to revolve around his name. Now, there was only the echo of footsteps on concrete and the steady clang of routine. Prison, for most, is an ending. For Joey, it became something else a long pause, a hard mirror, a test of what remained when everything else was stripped away.

He had entered those walls with the same calm defiance that had carried him through every storm. To those watching, he looked unbroken, almost indifferent. But prison has a way of peeling back layers. Behind the smile, behind the trademark confidence, there was reflection not regret exactly, but reckoning.

The Reality of Confinement

Life inside wasn't glamorous. There were no tailored suits, no soft lights, no admiring eyes. Days blurred into one another, ruled by the same rhythms: wake, count, eat, work, wait. Freedom became memory; time became the enemy. But Joey adapted quickly. He had grown up in a world that prized discipline, loyalty, and toughness traits that served him well behind bars.

He rose early, kept himself fit, and kept to a small circle. He didn't complain, didn't crumble, didn't court sympathy. To the men around him, he was steady, approachable, but private. He carried himself with the quiet confidence of someone who had already faced worse on the outside.

There were those who expected him to fade, to become just another forgotten figure behind the fence. But Joey never let that happen. His name, his reputation those things carried weight, even in confinement. Respect followed him, not because of fear, but because of composure.

In a world where tempers ruled and pride could be dangerous, Joey's calmness became his strength. He spoke little, listened often, and gave advice without arrogance. Those who met him during those years described him as focused, surprisingly humble, and unshaken.

He learned to treat time like a resource something to be spent wisely. Reading became habit, reflection became ritual. He studied not only history and philosophy but also business and law. He read about leadership, negotiation, and endurance. To the outside world, he was gone. But inside, he was quietly evolving.

Letters, Faith, and Family

If there was one thing that kept Joey grounded, it was connection. He never cut himself off from the people who mattered. Letters became lifelines handwritten words passed through metal and paper that carried warmth into cold corridors.

His wife and daughters remained his greatest anchors. Their voices reminded him that beyond the walls, there was still love, still a world that believed in him not as a symbol, but as a man. He wrote back constantly not to dwell on loss, but to remind them, and himself, that he was still the same person, still present, still alive.

Faith also grew stronger in those years. It wasn't loud or performative, but personal a quiet conversation between him and something larger than the bars around him. He attended services, prayed privately, and began to see time as a chance to rebuild from within. Faith, family, and routine became the foundation that kept him steady.

The Quiet Influence

Inside prison, influence doesn't come from wealth or fame it comes from respect. And respect can't be faked. Joey earned it not by force, but by example. He didn't posture or play the role of a tough guy. He offered calm where others offered noise, composure where others lost control.

He looked after younger inmates when he could, offered words of perspective, and discouraged trouble that led nowhere. He understood that real power wasn't in dominating others, but in surviving with dignity.

Some of the men around him came and went. Others stayed and became quiet friends. For many, Joey represented something rare someone who had lived through storms and still walked with purpose. His presence, even in silence, reminded them that identity survives confinement.

The guards respected him, too. He followed the rules, didn't stir conflict, didn't trade favors or challenge authority. He carried himself with the same composure that once disarmed journalists. And in that way, Joey Merlino managed something remarkable he kept his reputation intact in a place designed to erase it.

The Outside World Keeps Watching

Even behind bars, Joey's name refused to vanish from the headlines. Journalists speculated about him, old associates spoke about him, and the public especially in Philadelphia continued to follow his story. He had become a symbol, a kind of myth that couldn't be confined by walls.

Every mention of him carried the same fascination: *What's Joey doing now? How is he handling it? Will he come back?*

To his frustration, rumors often outpaced truth. People imagined secret influence, whispered about control from the inside. In reality, Joey was focused on surviving the present, not plotting the future. Still, the fascination proved something: even in silence, he held the world's attention.

The media painted him as the last of a certain kind the charismatic outlaw, the man who smiled through scandal and refused to bend. They didn't see the long nights, the quiet moments, the hard work of keeping one's soul intact. They saw the legend, not the man. But Joey understood that too. He had built that legend, and now it lived a life of its own.

Moments of Reflection

Time changes a man, especially when it slows down. Inside, Joey had more of it than he'd ever wanted. He used it to look backward, not in regret, but in understanding. He thought about South

Philadelphia the narrow streets, the smell of fresh bread, the Sunday dinners where loyalty was first taught. He remembered his father's lessons, the people he'd lost, the nights when he had thought himself invincible.

There were regrets, of course, but they were quiet private recognitions of choices made too quickly or trusts placed too freely. But he didn't dwell on what couldn't be changed. His focus remained forward: survival, integrity, and peace.

He began to write in journals. Not confessions, not declarations, but thoughts fragments of perspective about loyalty, power, image, and life. To those who knew him, that wasn't surprising. Joey had always been a thinker behind the charm, someone who understood how image shaped perception. Now, he was rethinking his own.

In those writings, he often came back to one theme: control. He had lost control of the narrative, of his freedom, but not of himself. And in a place where control was the rarest commodity, that was victory.

The Reputation That Endured

In time, Joey became something of a legend inside as well. Even those who didn't know his past knew his presence. His discipline, his calm, his unwavering dignity those traits became his new form of power.

He never bragged, never pretended, never tried to live off the stories that swirled around his name. Instead, he lived by quiet principle. He kept his tone polite, his word solid, and his focus sharp. The older inmates respected him; the younger ones admired him. He didn't play politics, didn't need protection. He had built his own kind of shield one made of reputation and restraint.

Every system has its hierarchy, and Joey found his place in this one not through fear, but through respect earned slowly. The men who came and went learned something from him how to hold on to who they were even when the world tried to define them otherwise.

Freedom Deferred

Years passed, slowly but steadily. The outside world changed in ways Joey couldn't have imagined. Technology advanced, the city moved on, and the names that once filled headlines faded into history. Yet his didn't. The world remembered him sometimes as a villain, sometimes as a folk hero, but always as Joey Merlino.

When the time for release finally came, it didn't arrive with fanfare. There were no parades, no flashing lights just the sound of a door unlocking, the feel of air that didn't belong to the institution. He walked out thinner, quieter, older but still recognizably himself.

Freedom, he discovered, was heavier than he remembered. The world outside was louder, faster, and more suspicious. Old friends reached out cautiously. Reporters hovered. Cameras appeared again, eager to capture the first smile of a man who had been silenced for years.

He smiled, of course that same steady grin that had once lit up newsstands across the country. But this time, it wasn't performance. It was gratitude. He had survived.

Beyond the Walls

What came after was not a return to the past but an evolution. Joey settled into life in Florida, far from the streets that had once defined him. He opened a restaurant, blending nostalgia with new beginnings a place where laughter replaced headlines, where the smell of grilled food replaced the sterile scent of confinement.

Customers came as much for the food as for the name. But Joey treated everyone the same polite, calm, focused on service, not stories. To those who expected arrogance or spectacle, he offered something else: peace.

He wasn't running from his past, but he wasn't reliving it either. He was building something quieter a new rhythm, a new kind of loyalty, a life that didn't need cameras or crowds to have meaning.

He spoke rarely about prison, but when he did, his words carried weight. He didn't glorify it or dramatize it. He spoke about endurance, about learning patience, about the importance of faith and family. He said that sometimes, losing everything teaches you what truly matters.

Resilience Redefined

People often asked how he kept his composure how he emerged from years behind bars still smiling, still measured. The answer, he once said, was simple: *"You don't let the time do you; you do the time."*

It was the same principle that had carried him through every challenge control what you can, let go of what you can't. That philosophy became the center of his post-prison life. He no longer chased attention; he valued privacy. The man who once filled front pages now preferred quiet dinners, golf outings, and long evenings with family.

Yet even as he sought peace, he remained a figure of fascination. People couldn't quite let go of the image the man who had once smiled through storms. But this time, Joey wasn't playing to them. He had learned that real strength doesn't need an audience.

The Man Beyond the Myth

In the end, what prison had given Joey was perspective. It stripped away illusion and left only truth. He saw how fragile loyalty could be, how quickly fame fades, and how easily stories are rewritten. But he also learned how strong identity can be when it's rooted in something real.

He emerged older, yes, but also lighter. The past was still there, but it no longer defined him. He had become something else not the outlaw, not the icon, but the survivor.

To those who met him afterward, he seemed at peace. The same sharp humor, the same confidence, but tempered now by reflection. He spoke of the importance of family, of making the most of each day, of finding meaning beyond reputation.

And in that sense, Joey Merlino became something no one expected a man transformed, not defeated.

He had lost freedom, time, and trust but never himself. Behind the walls, he had rediscovered the essence of who he was: loyal, disciplined, enduring. The years had taken much, but they had also refined him.

The world may remember him for the headlines, the trials, the tapes. But those who truly knew him remember something else the resilience, the grace under pressure, the refusal to break.

Because even behind bars, Joey Merlino found a way to live beyond them.

Chapter 10

The Comeback Kid

When the gates finally opened and Joey Merlino stepped out into the light, it wasn't freedom that struck him first it was silence. The kind of silence that comes after years of noise, of footsteps echoing in cellblocks, of metal doors clanging shut behind him. The air outside felt different softer, lighter yet heavier with expectation. The world had changed since he went in, but in a way, Joey hadn't. He still had that swagger, that confident tilt of the chin, that half-smile that could disarm or deflect. But beneath it all was something quieter a man who had learned to adapt.

Prison hadn't broken him; it had reshaped him. It taught him patience, taught him how to read people without a word. It stripped away illusions and left behind only what was real: reputation, resilience, and resolve. Joey wasn't stepping back into the same Philadelphia he'd left. He was stepping into a world that had evolved digital, faster, unforgiving. But Joey had always been quick on his feet. If life was a game, he still knew how to play.

The Return to the Streets

The first few weeks were a blur of familiar faces and cautious embraces. Old friends came by, some out of loyalty, others out of curiosity. Everyone wanted to know the same thing what was next for Skinny Joey?

He didn't rush to answer. For the first time in years, he took his time. He reconnected with his family, especially his wife and daughters, whose strength had anchored him through the darkest nights. They had weathered the storms the headlines, the speculation, the whispers and stood by him. That kind of loyalty wasn't just earned; it was sacred.

Philadelphia still buzzed with his name, but Joey had learned to move differently. The bravado was tempered with reflection. He had spent years learning how to survive behind bars, and now, survival meant something new staying relevant without crossing lines.

Reporters waited, cameras hovered, and his name still carried the same mix of fascination and fear. To some, he was a relic of the past a man out of step with modern times. To others, he was proof that legends don't fade; they adapt.

And Joey, ever the strategist, saw an opportunity to rewrite his story.

Rebranding the Legend

If prison was a test of endurance, then freedom was a test of reinvention. Joey wasn't interested in going backward he wanted to move forward, but on his own terms. The idea was simple: take control of the narrative. For years, the press had defined him, turned his name into a headline. Now, he wanted to define himself.

It started subtly a few interviews, some public appearances. He was calm, even charming. The suits were still sharp, the smile still knowing, but the tone was different. He wasn't the loud, camera-loving figure of the 1990s anymore. This was a man who had learned how to hold a room without raising his voice.

Then came the ventures. Joey saw business not as an escape, but as evolution. Restaurants, real estate, connections in Florida the seeds of a legitimate life that could outlive his past. It wasn't easy; there were always questions, always suspicions. But for once, the attention wasn't just about what he'd done it was about what he might do next.

Even skeptics admitted that his charisma was undeniable. The same qualities that once drew people to him confidence, humor, loyalty still worked, only now they were redirected. Joey wasn't hiding from his past, but he wasn't living in it either.

He understood the value of perception better than anyone. In a world obsessed with stories, Joey was rewriting his own one smile, one appearance, one business deal at a time.

The Weight of a Name

Still, being Joey Merlino came with baggage. The name carried history power, controversy, myth. No matter how much he tried to live quietly, the world around him refused to let go. Every phone call, every dinner meeting, every photo taken with an old friend became fodder for speculation.

He knew it came with the territory. The FBI still watched, reporters still wrote, and people still whispered. But Joey didn't flinch. He had learned long ago that image was both his curse and his crown.

Sometimes, when he walked through South Philly, he could feel the eyes on him some admiring, some judging. But he walked with the same calm rhythm, the same steady confidence. Inside, he'd changed, but outwardly, he remained the same Joey the city had always known composed, deliberate, untouchable in spirit.

To his critics, he was still the man who refused to fade. To his supporters, he was proof that survival wasn't about denial it was about resilience.

And for Joey, that was enough.

The New Game

What most didn't see was how carefully Joey moved. The charm that once disarmed adversaries was now used to disarm perception. He understood the modern world of optics how a picture, a headline, or a tweet could shape a story before he ever spoke a word.

So he stayed smart. He stayed visible, but never too visible. He chose his appearances wisely, spoke in measured tones, smiled often, and said little. Every move was deliberate, every word filtered through a quiet awareness that the world was still watching waiting for him to slip.

But Joey had no intention of slipping. Not this time. He'd played too many games, seen too many traps. His focus now was on legacy not just survival, but transformation.

Behind closed doors, he was more thoughtful than people imagined. He talked about life, about time lost and time regained. He reflected on the meaning of loyalty, of friendship, of family. The man who once lived fast now lived with purpose. The fire hadn't gone out it had simply learned to burn slower, steadier.

Fame Reimagined

Then came the call a producer, a documentary, an opportunity to tell his story on screen. Joey knew the risks. The media had always twisted his image, but he also knew that storytelling had power.

The world loved him because he was real, because he wasn't polished or pretending. He had lived the kind of life people read about but rarely understood. And now, in an era where authenticity ruled, Joey Merlino once the poster boy for excess became something new: a symbol of survival.

Netflix, news outlets, podcasts everyone wanted a piece of the story. The line between myth and man blurred again, but this time, Joey was in control. He didn't need to prove innocence or guilt; he only needed to be himself.

And in a world where image is everything, authenticity is the rarest currency of all.

The Measure of Redemption

For Joey, redemption was never about apologies or headlines. It wasn't about convincing others to forgive; it was about learning to live without regret. He'd made choices, taken risks, and paid the price.

Now, every day was a quiet declaration that he was still standing.

Some nights, he'd sit outside the Florida air thick and warm and think about the long road behind him. The faces, the fights, the victories, the losses. He didn't dwell on them. He carried them like chapters in a book only he could fully read.

The man who once chased chaos now cherished calm. The man who once lived for attention now preferred peace. But through it all, Joey remained Joey sharp, magnetic, unbreakable in spirit.

He was no longer the outlaw prince of Philadelphia. He was something rarer: a man who had outlived his legend.

And as he looked toward whatever came next the business ventures, the documentaries, the quiet dinners with old friends he carried the same lesson that had guided him through every storm:

You can't control the story people tell about you. You can only control how you live it.

Chapter 11

Skinny Joey's Cheesesteaks

It started, as so many of Joey Merlino's ideas did, with a spark a conversation over coffee, a laugh, a passing comment that became a plan. He had been back in the world for a while, keeping a low profile, moving carefully, thinking strategically. The name "Skinny Joey" still carried weight, but Joey wanted to give it new meaning something that wasn't tied to headlines, trials, or whispers. He wanted it attached to something people could taste, something tangiblc.

And what could be more Philadelphia more honest, more real than a cheesesteak?

For Joey, the idea was more than business; it was symbolism. A cheesesteak wasn't just a sandwich. It was the city itself gritty, proud, flavorful, unpretentious. It was South Philly on a roll, served hot. And for a man who had lived every flavor of life sweet success, bitter loss, spicy controversy it was the perfect metaphor for reinvention.

The Recipe for Redemption

When Joey first shared his plan, most people smiled and shrugged. Some thought it was a joke that a man once at the center of a media storm wanted to open a food stand. But those who knew him best weren't surprised. Joey had always been about connection with people, with community, with the energy of a room.

"Food brings people together," he told a friend one afternoon. "And if there's one thing I've learned, it's that people love a good story and a better sandwich."

He wasn't wrong.

The restaurant concept came together piece by piece a mix of classic Philly tradition and modern flair.

Joey didn't want gimmicks or flash. He wanted something authentic, something that reflected who he was now. The name Skinny Joey's Cheesesteaks struck the perfect balance: familiar, catchy, and rooted in his identity yet playful enough to invite curiosity.

The vision was simple: good food, good company, no pretense. A place where anyone from old friends to curious newcomers could walk in, grab a cheesesteak, and walk out satisfied.

But underneath that simplicity was meticulous planning. Joey studied menus, tested recipes, compared bread rolls from different bakeries, and talked to chefs who knew the city's flavor inside out. He wasn't just putting his name on a sign he was crafting an experience.

The Business of Belief

Starting a business with a name like Joey Merlino's wasn't easy. There were raised eyebrows, rumors, and questions. But Joey knew that controversy wasn't his enemy perception was. And perception could be managed.

So, he leaned into transparency. No bravado, no defensiveness just quiet confidence. When asked why he chose to open a cheesesteak spot, his answer was disarmingly simple:

"Because everybody loves a good sandwich. And I love Philly."

The authenticity worked.

People came not just for the food, but for the story. They wanted to see what Joey would do next, to witness his next act. And when they bit into that perfectly seasoned, sizzling cheesesteak, they found something unexpected not the ghost of a past life, but the warmth of a man who understood community.

Joey made sure every detail reflected that. The shop wasn't designed to feel fancy or corporate. It was local, inviting, honest with photos of Philadelphia's skyline on the walls and a playlist that mixed Sinatra with Springsteen.

Behind the counter, the energy was alive. Joey didn't hide in an office; he mingled with customers, cracked jokes, shook hands, asked how the food was. The charisma that once charmed reporters and socialites now filled the air with laughter and ease.

A Name, Reimagined

Of course, the name "Skinny Joey" still turned heads. It carried decades of stories some true, some exaggerated, some invented. But now, it was on menus, aprons, and takeaway bags. The name that once symbolized danger now represented flavor.

And that was Joey's quiet genius. He didn't deny who he'd been; he simply redirected the meaning.

In interviews, he spoke about the restaurant as a second chance not in the sense of starting over, but in redefining legacy. "People will always talk," he said with a smile. "So, give them something good to talk about."

That line stuck. It wasn't just a quote; it became the brand's soul.

Soon, the buzz spread. Locals came for the food; travelers came for the story. And everyone left with something to say. Joey's personality sharp, funny, unexpectedly warm lingered as much as the taste of onions sizzling on the grill.

For the first time in decades, "Skinny Joey" wasn't a tabloid headline. It was a business name one that stood for effort, quality, and connection.

The Taste of Transformation

The menu was built on authenticity. Each sandwich had its own rhythm the roll slightly crisp, the meat tender, the cheese melting just right. Joey took pride in the details. He'd walk through the kitchen, check on staff, taste sauces, adjust seasoning.

He was hands-on, but not controlling. He treated the place like family a living, breathing reflection of his journey.

"Keep it simple," he'd say. "Keep it honest. People can taste fake."

And they could. Customers felt it the sincerity behind the operation. Joey wasn't pretending to be someone else. He was exactly who he appeared to be: a man who had lived enough life for three people and still had the humor to make you laugh while serving a sandwich.

The restaurant became a hub a meeting point between past and present. Construction workers, lawyers, tourists, and locals all shared tables. Conversations drifted from sports to music to city gossip. Joey moved between them all with the same easy rhythm, a man fully at home in his new chapter.

Challenges and Perseverance

Not everything came easy. Running a restaurant meant long hours, thin margins, and constant work. Joey faced setbacks supply issues, staffing turnover, economic shifts. And there were always those who doubted, who assumed the venture would collapse under its own curiosity.

But Joey thrived under pressure. He'd faced worse and survived. Compared to courtrooms and cages, running a restaurant was a blessing.

Whenever problems arose, he met them with the same mindset that had carried him through life: adapt, adjust, and never back down. He saw each obstacle not as failure, but as part of the grind part of the proof that redemption wasn't a headline but a daily choice.

The same resilience that once kept him strong in far darker places now fueled his business spirit.

The Flavor of Legacy

Months turned into years, and the restaurant took on a life of its own. For Joey, it wasn't about profit as much as presence. Each customer who walked through the door represented something bigger a chance to rewrite perception, to replace myth with reality.

He understood that success wasn't about escaping the past; it was about transforming it.

Skinny Joey's Cheesesteaks became more than a food spot it was a statement. A living reminder that reinvention isn't about erasing your history; it's about seasoning it with experience and serving it back to the world, better than before.

And so, when people walked out of the restaurant, licking cheese from their fingers, smiling at the memory of Joey cracking a joke near the counter, they didn't think about the old stories. They thought about the new one the man who turned a name into a flavor, and a past into a brand.

Chapter 12

The Podcast Persona

It began, fittingly, not in a studio but at a dinner table a small group of friends laughing over stories that could fill a hundred books. Joey Merlino was in his element: charming, sharp, and full of timing that made even the most serious moments feel like legends retold. Someone, between laughter and dessert, said what everyone was thinking:

"Joey, you need a podcast."

At first, he brushed it off. A podcast? Him? It sounded too modern, too loud, too open. But the more he thought about it, the more it made sense. For years, other people had told his story reporters, prosecutors, filmmakers, even former friends. They'd taken pieces of his life, twisted them into headlines, and sold the legend of "Skinny Joey" to audiences hungry for myth.

Maybe, he thought, it was time to take his voice back.

The Age of the Microphone

The world had changed since Joey first became a household name. Gone were the smoky backrooms and late-night whispers. Now, everything happened on screens in podcasts, on social media, through snippets of sound that spread faster than any rumor could.

Joey had spent most of his life mastering real conversation: eye contact, tone, rhythm. The digital age had different rules, but the essence was the same control the narrative or be controlled by it.

When he finally agreed to the idea, he did it his way. No gimmicks, no fake dramatics, no attempts to play someone he wasn't. He'd sit behind a microphone, maybe pour a glass of wine, and talk. About life, loyalty, the streets, family, mistakes, resilience the themes that had shaped him.

The podcast wasn't about glamorizing the past. It was about reclaiming truth from exaggeration.

And people listened.

Finding His Voice Again

The first few episodes were rough around the edges unfiltered, candid, magnetic. Joey's tone carried the rhythm of South Philly: confident, witty, and street-smart, but with the weight of reflection. Listeners could hear the layers the humor, the regret, the pride, the peace.

He didn't name names. He didn't sensationalize. He told stories with meaning about loyalty, choices, and the shifting world around him. It was less about what happened and more about what it taught him.

That was what made the podcast powerful. It wasn't about the mob; it was about the man.

Each episode drew thousands of listeners some longtime followers, others curious newcomers who had only heard his name in documentaries. They were surprised to find not a caricature, but a man who spoke plainly, who could make them laugh one minute and reflect deeply the next.

Joey's natural rhythm translated beautifully to audio. He had the rare ability to make listeners feel like they were sitting across from him at a café, hearing secrets told with trust.

It wasn't performance; it was presence.

The Digital Tightrope

But stepping into the digital world wasn't without risk. For someone who had lived decades under scrutiny, every word carried weight. A casual phrase could become a headline; a misinterpreted story could be twisted into controversy.

Joey knew it. He had learned long ago that silence was often safer. But silence also meant surrender letting others keep painting the picture of him.

The podcast became a tightrope between transparency and protection.

He spoke carefully, never crossing lines, always aware that the world was still listening just as it always had been. But now, he was the one holding the microphone.

And that, for Joey, was freedom.

The show's format was simple: conversation. No scripts, no producers dictating flow. Sometimes, he'd bring on guests old friends, local business owners, musicians, even former critics. The tone was open, grounded, and authentic.

The episodes weren't about drama. They were about perspective a man who had lived through extremes, now reflecting on them with surprising calm.

Social Media, Real Talk

Alongside the podcast, Joey began to explore social media. Platforms like Instagram and X (formerly Twitter) gave him a direct line to the public. For the first time in his life, there were no intermediaries no reporters, no lawyers, no publicists.

He posted pictures of his restaurant, short videos promoting new episodes, and occasional glimpses into daily life. He smiled in most of them relaxed, casual, confident. Gone was the guarded stare of old newspaper clippings.

And people loved it.

The comments were a mix of admiration, nostalgia, and curiosity. Some thanked him for his honesty; others said they finally felt they knew the real Joey.

His humor dry and disarming shone through in every caption. He'd answer questions, share quotes, crack jokes about sports or food, and remind people that life, at its core, was simple: "Work hard. Stay loyal. Keep moving."

Social media, once the enemy of privacy, became his greatest ally in reclaiming authenticity.

Rewriting Omertà

In the old world, silence was sacred. The code of omertà the vow of silence had defined entire generations of men. But Joey's silence had long been used against him, twisted into implication.

This new chapter wasn't about breaking that code. It was about redefining it.

He wasn't exposing secrets; he was exposing truths about life the cost of loyalty, the meaning of freedom, the way time changes perspective. He wasn't betraying anyone; he was betraying the caricature.

And that, in a world where everyone had an opinion about him, was a revolutionary act.

In a way, Joey had always been a communicator just never in front of a mic. The podcast gave him a platform where he didn't have to shout to be heard. His calm tone, measured pauses, and unexpected insight made listeners stop and think.

He wasn't asking for sympathy. He was offering understanding.

The Art of Storytelling

As the podcast grew, it evolved from conversation into something more profound a reflection of legacy. Each episode was like a chapter of a memoir told out loud, a slow, deliberate reclaiming of his life's story.

He spoke about family dinners, about South Philly summers, about loss and loyalty, about learning to live with your past without letting it define you.

Sometimes he'd laugh mid-story, breaking into that signature grin that listeners could almost hear. Other times, he'd go quiet, letting silence fill the space. Those pauses said as much as his words.

He wasn't preaching; he was remembering.

And in those moments, even people who had never walked his path felt connected. Because his stories weren't really about crime or power they were about being human.

The New Kind of Influence

In time, "The Skinny Joey Show" as fans nicknamed it became a cultural curiosity. Journalists who once wrote about him as a figure of the past were now quoting him as a voice of reflection. Younger generations, who only knew him through documentaries, discovered someone more complex a man who owned his story and refused to let anyone else narrate it.

Podcast platforms featured him under categories like "True Life," "Motivation," and "Cultural History." Joey laughed at that. "They used to call me a problem," he'd say. "Now they call me content."

But beneath the humor was truth. He'd found a way to turn the loudest years of his life into lessons to show that survival isn't just about staying alive; it's about evolving.

The Voice That Outlasts the Noise

Every recording session ended the same way. The microphone would click off, the room would go quiet, and Joey would sit for a moment thoughtful, still.

He had lived a life most couldn't imagine. And now, instead of being spoken about, he was speaking for himself.

The irony wasn't lost on him: after years of being pursued by microphones, he now owned one. After decades of others telling his story, he was finally telling it in his own words unfiltered, unafraid, and unapologetically real.

In the end, that was Joey Merlino's greatest reinvention not as a figure from the past, but as a voice for the present.

And as his closing line in one of his most listened-to episodes captured perfectly:

"People say I changed. Maybe I did. Or maybe I just stopped letting other people talk for me."

Chapter 13

Shelved or Still Standing?

In Philadelphia, silence still speaks louder than words. The city that raised Joey Merlino hums with whispers some nostalgic, some speculative, all impossible to prove. Every few years, his name resurfaces in headlines, in podcasts, in neighborhood gossip, like a familiar song that refuses to fade from the air. People still ask the same question, though they rarely say it aloud:

Is Joey Merlino still standing, or has he finally stepped away for good?

The truth, as always with Joey, lives somewhere in the quiet space between perception and reality.

The Weight of a Name

Decades after his rise, the name "Joey Merlino" still stirs something visceral in Philadelphia. It's not just nostalgia it's legend. To some, he remains a symbol of the old ways, a reminder of loyalty, presence, and grit in a city that has changed beyond recognition. To others, he's a ghost of another era someone who belongs to a world that should have vanished with it.

But to those who know him or think they do Joey is neither ghost nor relic. He's survivor and strategist, someone who long ago learned that power doesn't always come from presence. Sometimes, it comes from patience.

He's not seen often in South Philly these days. His life has grown quieter, more controlled. Yet the stillness only deepens the mystery.

The whispers say he's retired. Others say he still moves pieces from behind the curtain, that his influence lingers in conversations between old friends, in favors repaid and names remembered. The truth is smaller, simpler but no less intriguing.

Joey Merlino learned that to stay standing, sometimes you have to step sideways, not forward.

Rumors in the Air

Philadelphia thrives on stories especially the kind that can't be confirmed. In diners, barber shops, and bars, people still lower their voices when his name comes up.

"I heard he's done with all that."
"I heard he's living quiet down south."
"I heard he still gets respect even from the young guys."

Each story contradicts the next, but that's how legends survive through uncertainty. Joey, always a master of perception, understands this better than anyone. The less he says, the more people talk.

And he doesn't correct them.

He lets the stories swirl like smoke, knowing that mystery is a kind of power in itself.

To those who've watched him for years, this silence isn't retreat. It's design. Joey knows that in a world where everyone talks too much, the man who stays silent controls the room.

The Codes That Never Die

To understand Joey today, you have to understand the world he came from a world built on codes, not contracts. Loyalty wasn't written down; it was lived. Trust wasn't given; it was earned. And betrayal, once committed, was eternal.

Even as society evolved, those rules quiet, unspoken never fully disappeared. They simply went underground, like roots under concrete. Joey carried them into every chapter of his life prison, family, business, even the restaurant. The codes weren't about crime; they were about character.

In interviews and on his podcast, he speaks of loyalty like it's sacred. He doesn't glorify it. He defines it. "You can't buy it," he says. "You either have it, or you don't."

Those who know him well say that's the real reason he still commands respect. Not because of what he did, but because of how he stood.

He didn't beg for sympathy. He didn't betray old ties to save himself. He served his time, kept his word, and walked out with his dignity intact. In a world that celebrates exposure, Joey's greatest rebellion is restraint.

Life in the Quiet Lane

These days, Joey's life looks deceptively simple. He splits time between Florida and the Northeast, keeping close to family and a tight circle of friends. He still carries that same calm presence the confidence that doesn't shout.

He plays golf. He eats well. He laughs often.

But beneath the calm, there's an edge the awareness that life, for him, will always be a kind of balancing act. He's too well-known to disappear, too self-aware to repeat history.

The men who once feared him now greet him warmly. The ones who envied him now study him. And the city that once judged him now treats him like an icon of its own complicated story flawed, fascinating, and impossible to erase.

Freedom, for Joey, isn't about invisibility. It's about choice choosing where to go, whom to see, when to speak, and when to smile and let people wonder.

Respect That Lasts

Ask around, and you'll hear it in every corner of Philadelphia: the respect for Joey Merlino endures. It's not fear. It's something quieter an acknowledgment that he played the game, survived the fallout, and somehow came out still walking tall.

He's not the brash young man of the '90s anymore. Time has smoothed the sharp edges, but the steel underneath remains.

Even those who never liked him admit it: Joey has what few ever achieve staying power.

In the streets, that's rarer than gold.

Because the truth about legends is this: they don't retire. They just evolve.

The Line Between Fact and Myth

In a digital world obsessed with proof, Joey remains the rare figure who thrives on ambiguity. Is he truly retired? Is he still connected? Does he still carry the same kind of influence he once did? No one really knows. And that's exactly how he wants it.

He exists somewhere between fact and folklore a living contradiction who's both here and not here, present and untouchable.

Documentaries, articles, and endless online speculation still circle around him, but none can quite pin him down. Every quote, every sighting, every public appearance becomes a Rorschach test people see what they want to see.

And Joey, ever the strategist, allows it.

He's long since stopped trying to control the narrative. Now, he simply embodies it.

Still Standing

If there's one truth that endures through the noise, it's this: Joey Merlino is still standing. Maybe not in the way people expect, but in the way that truly matters.

He's not chasing power anymore he's chasing peace. He's not fighting for control he's found it in stillness.

In a city that changes every season, his name remains, steady as brick and marble. Not because of fame or infamy, but because of endurance. Because he represents something that can't be easily erased the last vestige of a code, a charisma, a time when reputation meant everything.

So when people ask where Joey Merlino stands today, the answer is both simple and profound:

He stands where he's always stood on his own terms.

Chapter 14

The Netflix Effect

For decades, Joey Merlino was a man whose story belonged to whispered conversations, courtroom transcripts, and the yellowed pages of old newspaper clippings. But then came the age of streaming when nostalgia, curiosity, and digital storytelling collided. Suddenly, what had once been hidden in the shadows found new life on glowing screens across the world.

When *Mob War: The Philadelphia Chronicles* dropped on Netflix, it didn't just resurrect a forgotten chapter of American organized crime it reignited the global fascination with Joey Merlino himself. Overnight, the man who once dodged cameras became the subject of cinematic close-ups, slow-motion reenactments, and podcast debates. For a new generation of viewers, Joey wasn't just a name in history. He was a character a legend reborn through the lens of Hollywood.

But as the buzz grew louder, one question began to echo through every online forum and newsroom: where does the truth end, and the show begin?

A Legend in High Definition

The first episode of *Mob War* opened with archival footage black-and-white shots of South Philadelphia streets, family-owned bakeries, and men in fedoras shaking hands under flickering streetlights. The narration was cinematic, almost poetic, describing the city as a "place where loyalty could build an empire and betrayal could end it in a heartbeat."

Then came the face that defined an era a young Joey Merlino, all swagger and style, flashing a grin that both charmed and unsettled. The show didn't shy away from his contradictions. It portrayed him as bold yet reckless, charismatic yet complicated, loyal yet always under fire.

For audiences around the world many of whom had never heard of Philadelphia's underworld the image was captivating. Here was a man who seemed to live between two worlds: one ruled by the codes of the street, the other by the rhythm of the spotlight.

The Netflix cameras did what the newspapers of the '90s couldn't they turned Joey's life into a cinematic experience, blending fact, rumor, and nostalgia into something that felt larger than truth itself.

When Hollywood Meets History

The creative team behind *Mob War* insisted the series was built on research, not romance. They scoured court records, old FBI reports, and local archives to paint a picture of the city's most volatile years. But the line between storytelling and journalism blurred the moment the show hit number one in the U.S.

Hollywood, after all, has a way of amplifying what's already dramatic.

Every conversation became sharper. Every gesture, a metaphor. Every piece of dialogue reconstructed to fit the emotional arc of the story. The result was gripping television and a whole new wave of public fascination with Joey Merlino.

Critics praised the show for its realism. Fans devoured the style, the soundtrack, the tension. But those who knew the real Joey or lived through those years watched with mixed emotions. They saw familiar streets and faces, yes, but they also saw how easily truth could be edited for entertainment.

It wasn't just about accuracy. It was about ownership of narrative.

Who gets to tell the story of a man still alive? Who decides which moments become canon, and which ones are buried beneath dramatic license?

For Joey, who had spent years trying to control how the world saw him, the Netflix effect was both a gift and a curse.

A Star Reborn Again

The docuseries turned Joey into a trending topic overnight. Social media lit up with old headlines, fan theories, and video essays dissecting his personality. TikTok edits played vintage photos of him against jazz soundtracks, calling him "the last real gangster."

YouTube channels broke down his interviews frame by frame, analyzing his expressions for hints of truth. Reddit threads filled with debates over whether he was a misunderstood businessman or the last of a dying breed.

What few realized was that Joey himself had long understood the game.

He had lived through every headline, every accusation, every moment of media hysteria. The Netflix version of him was just another reflection polished, dramatized, and commodified. But it wasn't the whole picture.

Those close to him said he watched the show quietly, neither angry nor flattered. He had learned long ago that once a story leaves your hands, it belongs to the audience.

"The public loves an image," he said once on his podcast. "They build you up, they tear you down, and if you're lucky they build you back again. The trick is not to take any of it personal."

Separating Fact from Fiction

The show's popularity also reignited a broader cultural debate: why does the world remain obsessed with the mythology of organized crime?

From *The Godfather* to *Goodfellas*, from podcasts to true-crime documentaries, audiences have always gravitated toward figures who embody both power and peril. Joey, with his charm and contradictions, fits that mold perfectly a man who once ruled headlines and now lives quietly in a world that can't stop talking about him.

But *Mob War* blurred the lines between truth and spectacle more than ever.

In one scene, it suggested alliances that never existed. In another, it dramatized betrayals that were never proven. Even the timeline bent under the weight of narrative convenience. But that's what made it watchable and what made the real-life players uneasy.

Philadelphia's old-timers shook their heads. "That ain't how it went," some muttered. Others shrugged and said, "Doesn't matter. People believe what they see."

And that's the real power of the Netflix effect perception becomes permanence.

The Man Behind the Screen

As the docuseries dominated charts and headlines, Joey's phone began buzzing again reporters, producers, old acquaintances. Everyone wanted a quote, a soundbite, a reaction.

He didn't give them one.

Instead, he doubled down on his own platform his podcast, where he spoke on his terms. He didn't dispute the show directly, but his tone made one thing clear: he was done letting other people define him.

He talked about discipline, loyalty, respect values that don't make for sensational television but form the backbone of a man trying to live a quiet life after years of chaos.

Listeners noticed the difference. The man behind the mic wasn't the brash figure of the '90s or the swaggering character onscreen. He was older, more reflective, sharper in his restraint.

Netflix might have revived his image, but Joey Merlino had already written his next chapter.

A Mirror for a Generation

In a strange way, *Mob War* did more than revive one man's legend it reflected society's evolving relationship with truth.

People no longer crave certainty; they crave story. They want characters who straddle right and wrong, loyalty and ambition. Joey's life offered all that in abundance, and the show packaged it perfectly for the streaming age cinematic, addictive, morally ambiguous.

But beneath the entertainment, there's a deeper current a fascination with authenticity. Joey's unfiltered honesty, his refusal to apologize for who he was, stands in stark contrast to a culture built on curated images. In that sense, he became a mirror, reflecting both the flaws and fantasies of a generation hungry for something real.

Hollywood's New Obsession

In the months following *Mob War's* release, production companies began circling. Scriptwriters pitched spinoffs. Studios discussed dramatized series inspired by Philadelphia's underworld. Joey's name became shorthand for a certain kind of charisma the anti-hero who never quite fits the mold.

But through it all, he stayed still.

He didn't sue. He didn't celebrate. He didn't chase another fifteen minutes of fame. He simply let the moment play out, watching the world rediscover him again.

To him, it was just another cycle. Fame burns fast; silence endures.

Legacy in Focus

When the credits rolled on the final episode, audiences were left with an image of Joey older, thoughtful, walking alone down a quiet Florida street. The camera lingered as if to ask: *What comes next?*

The answer, perhaps, lies beyond the frame.

Because the Netflix effect didn't change Joey Merlino it reminded the world why he mattered in the first place.

He wasn't just a figure from the past. He was proof that charisma and code can outlast chaos.

And while millions watched his story unfold through a Hollywood lens, those who really knew him smiled quietly. They understood the truth that no show could fully capture that Joey's greatest act wasn't surviving the mob or the media.

It was surviving both and still walking tall when the credits faded to black.

Chapter 15

The Last Mob Star

There are certain names that linger long after the smoke clears names that outlive the headlines, the trials, the stories that shaped them. Joey Merlino is one of those names. Not because he was the most powerful, or the most feared, but because he represented something rare the bridge between two fading worlds. One built on silence, loyalty, and tradition. The other on fame, spectacle, and digital noise.

He didn't belong entirely to either. Yet, somehow, he became the embodiment of both.

As the cameras fade and the decades stretch, Joey Merlino remains what few ever become a symbol. Not just of the Philadelphia underworld, but of transformation itself. His name has become shorthand for charisma under fire, for loyalty tested by time, and for the quiet rebellion of a man who refuses to let others write his ending.

He is, in every sense of the phrase, *the last mob star.*

A Life Lived Between Eras

Joey Merlino was born into a world already half-vanished. The old codes still existed respect, discretion, family first but they were cracking under the weight of a changing America. The generation before him had lived by silence; his generation was raised in the era of exposure.

By the time Joey came of age, television and tabloids had turned crime into entertainment, and fame into a form of power. What once hid in whispers now flashed across screens. The underworld wasn't secret anymore; it was spectacle.

And Joey, whether by instinct or inevitability, walked right into the center of it.

He didn't run from cameras he smiled for them. He didn't bury his personality behind shadows he wore it proudly. He understood what few of his predecessors ever could: image could be as powerful as influence.

That understanding made him controversial, but it also made him unforgettable.

The Birth of the Mob Celebrity

There had been notorious men before him Gotti, Lansky, Capone each commanding a different era's attention. But Joey was the first to emerge in an age where charisma counted as much as control.

The '90s made him more than a figure of crime pages; they made him a pop-culture curiosity. He dressed with flair, spoke with charm, and carried himself with a confidence that unsettled both law enforcement and admirers. Reporters called him "the John Gotti of Philadelphia," but the comparison was too simple.

Where Gotti embodied excess and defiance, Joey represented transition a man who knew the game was ending but played it like an artist refusing to fade from stage.

He became a paradox: both the modern face of an old institution and the first sign of its cultural evolution.

The Media's Love Affair with Myth

Part of Joey's lasting allure comes from how the media could never quite define him. Was he a criminal? A celebrity? A man trying to outlive his past?

Every profile, every documentary, every online theory tried to categorize him and every time, he slipped through the labels.

Because Joey wasn't just a product of his choices. He was a reflection of society's obsession with duality the good and the bad, the sinner and the survivor, the man who played by rules even as the world changed around him.

The media turned his life into an ongoing series of cliffhangers. Even in quiet years, the fascination never died. A candid photograph, a brief appearance, a cryptic podcast comment each one reignited the narrative.

And Joey, always deliberate, never gave more than a hint. He understood that mystery was his masterpiece.

The Meaning of the Mob Star

To call Joey Merlino "the last mob star" isn't just about crime or celebrity it's about timing.

He rose at the intersection of two dying traditions: the fading world of organized brotherhood and the rise of media as spectacle. The first prized silence; the second demanded noise.

Joey learned to walk that line. He respected the code but recognized the power of the lens. He never glorified what he did, but he never denied it either. In a world where truth is often rewritten, his greatest rebellion was transparency telling just enough, but never everything.

In that balance, he became something entirely new not just a figure of the underworld, but a cultural artifact. The last of an era that could be both feared and admired.

Legacy Beyond Crime

Time has a way of sanding down the rough edges of memory. What remains isn't the fear or the rumors it's the impact.

Joey Merlino's legacy today isn't about law enforcement records or courtroom verdicts. It's about endurance, charisma, and reinvention. He showed that even in the most rigid structures whether the mob or the media identity can evolve.

The man who once stood at the center of Philadelphia's chaos now sits at the crossroads of culture and caution. He's studied by journalists, discussed by podcasters, admired by filmmakers. His story has become shorthand for transformation for the art of surviving without surrendering your sense of self.

And perhaps that's what separates him from every name that came before. Others sought power. Joey found presence.

A World That No Longer Exists

The codes that raised Joey have vanished from modern streets. The brotherhoods have fractured, the alliances scattered. The digital age has replaced loyalty with likes, and secrecy with streams.

But even in this new landscape, Joey's story resonates because it speaks to something timeless. Beneath the headlines and history lies a universal truth: every man is measured by how he endures change.

He may be the last of his kind, but his relevance endures because his struggle mirrors everyone's the battle to stay authentic in a world obsessed with performance.

And that's what makes his story more than nostalgia. It makes it a study in survival.

Between Legend and Legacy

Ask ten people who Joey Merlino is, and you'll get ten different answers. A survivor. A businessman. A family man. A relic. A reformer.

But maybe that's the point. Legends aren't meant to be singular they're mirrors. They reflect what each generation needs to see.

To some, he's a warning. To others, he's inspiration. To all, he's unforgettable.

His journey from the backstreets of South Philly to the bright glare of the world's attention captures more than the end of an era. It captures the evolution of reputation itself.

He's proof that even when the system collapses, the spirit can endure.

The Message That Remains

In the end, Joey Merlino's story isn't just about crime, or even fame. It's about identity the battle to remain whole when the world keeps trying to divide you into pieces.

He's lived the cost of loyalty, the price of attention, and the peace of endurance. He's seen both the best and worst of what power brings. And through it all, he's never stopped being himself unapologetically, imperfectly, authentically.

The last mob star didn't fade into obscurity. He transformed into something more enduring a man who outlasted his myth, who learned that real strength isn't dominance, but definition.

Because while the mob may be gone, and the glamour may have dimmed, one truth remains clear:

Joey Merlino stands as the final echo of a world that once ruled the streets and the first symbol of a new kind of legacy that rules the mind.

Conclusion

The Man Who Wouldn't Disappear

There are stories that fade with time the ones that live and die in newspaper archives, in court records, in rumor. And then there are stories that refuse to disappear. Stories that stretch across decades, through chaos and calm, reshaping themselves until they become part of the culture itself. Joey Merlino's story belongs to that second kind.

He didn't just survive history he outlasted it.

His name has moved from the crime pages to the streaming age, from courtroom sketches to podcast headlines, from whispers in South Philly cafés to global conversations about fame, loyalty, and identity. Yet through every transformation, one thing has remained constant: the world never stopped watching him.

And maybe that's the heart of his legacy not the controversy, not the myth, but the endurance.

The Price of Being Seen

In America, fame is its own kind of trial. It can elevate or expose, heal or destroy. Joey Merlino understood that early. Long before the Netflix cameras or the social media chatter, he learned that the moment you step into the public eye, your life no longer belongs entirely to you.

He lived through the fever of attention the flashing cameras, the front-page headlines, the endless speculation. He also lived through the silence that followed, when the world moved on to new scandals and new stars.

But even then, he never really vanished.

Because Joey wasn't just a man who lived through fame he was a man who understood it. He knew that image, once created, becomes a living thing. It can't be erased, only redefined. And so, instead of fighting the myth, he learned to live beside it.

He didn't chase redemption. He chose reinvention.

That's what separates him from so many who came before and after.

The Mirror of a Nation

In many ways, Joey's story mirrors America's own evolution from grit to glamor, from loyalty to image, from substance to spectacle. His life traces the shift from the analog world of reputation to the digital world of recognition.

He began as a neighborhood figure, defined by his roots and his relationships. Over time, he became a national fascination a man who turned into both character and commentary.

Through him, America saw its own contradictions reflected back: our love for rebellion and our craving for redemption, our fascination with danger and our desire for control.

We turned his life into headlines because it represented something deeper the tension between authenticity and appearance, between who we are and who the world says we are.

In that sense, Joey Merlino became more than a figure of crime or controversy. He became a mirror one that showed us how easily admiration and judgment can share the same face.

From Chaos to Clarity

The Joey Merlino of today is not the man who once walked the crowded streets of South Philadelphia, drawing stares and stories wherever he went. Time changes everything, even legends.

He's older now, quieter. The sharp edges of his youth have softened into reflection. The man who once lived for the thrill of movement now values stillness. But beneath that calm, there remains a flicker of the fire that made him who he is confidence without arrogance, pride without performance.

He no longer needs to prove anything. His survival speaks louder than any statement could.

What began as a life defined by noise has settled into one defined by choice. He decides when to speak, when to retreat, when to let the story unfold without him. And that in an era addicted to constant visibility might be the boldest act of all.

The Power of Reinvention

Joey Merlino's greatest strength has never been intimidation or influence it's been his ability to adapt without losing his essence.

From the streets to the headlines, from prison cells to restaurant tables, from courtroom drama to podcast microphones, he's shown a rare kind of resilience the power to keep evolving while staying true to his core.

Each version of Joey reflects a chapter in America's changing fascination with fame:

The '90s outlaw, living large and unfiltered.

The 2000s survivor, tested but unbroken.

The 2010s businessman, turning infamy into industry.

The 2020s icon, a living relic of authenticity in a curated world.

Through it all, he's remained unmistakably himself calm, charming, deliberate. Never running from the past, but never imprisoned by it either.

His reinvention isn't about denial. It's about endurance.

The Legacy That Lingers

Joey Merlino's story ends not with a final act, but with a question: how does a man live after becoming his own legend?

For most, fame fades into nostalgia. But Joey's legend feels alive not because of crime or controversy, but because of what it represents: survival through transformation.

In him, people see the last echoes of something old and the first signs of something new. He's a reminder that charisma still matters, that loyalty still means something, and that even in a world addicted to exposure, mystery has its place.

His life isn't just a chronicle of events. It's a statement that even when the world changes, there are some people who never truly disappear.

Still Watching, Still Standing

Today, when his name trends online or his image flashes across a screen, it's no longer about scandal. It's about legacy.

The fascination endures because it's not just about who Jocy was, but what he symbolizes: the tension between loyalty and freedom, myth and man, performance and truth.

He's the rare figure who has lived through every cycle of public obsession and emerged still recognizable, still relevant, still unshaken.

And maybe that's why the story refuses to end.

Because Joey Merlino the man, the myth, the survivor isn't just a chapter in history. He's the last reflection of a world that once prized loyalty, charisma, and defiance in equal measure.

He is, and always will be, the man who wouldn't disappear.

www.ingramcontent.com/pod-product-compliance
Ingram Content Group UK Ltd.
Pitfield, Milton Keynes, MK11 3LW, UK
UKHW020718201125
9079UKWH00023B/330